SwiftUI for Absolute Beginners

Program Controls and Views for iPhone, iPad, and Mac Apps

Jayant Varma

Apress®

SwiftUI for Absolute Beginners: Program Controls and Views for iPhone, iPad, and Mac Apps

Jayant Varma
Melbourne, VIC, Australia

ISBN-13 (pbk): 978-1-4842-5515-5
https://doi.org/10.1007/978-1-4842-5516-2

ISBN-13 (electronic): 978-1-4842-5516-2

Managing Director, Apress Media LLC: Welmoed Spahr
Acquisitions Editor: Aaron Black
Development Editor: James Markham
Coordinating Editor: Jessica Vakili

Distributed to the book trade worldwide by Springer Science+Business Media New York, 233 Spring Street, 6th Floor, New York, NY 10013. Phone 1-800-SPRINGER, fax (201) 348-4505, e-mail orders-ny@springer-sbm.com, or visit www.springeronline.com. Apress Media, LLC is a California LLC and the sole member (owner) is Springer Science + Business Media Finance Inc (SSBM Finance Inc). SSBM Finance Inc is a **Delaware** corporation.

For information on translations, please e-mail rights@apress.com, or visit http://www.apress.com/rights-permissions.

Apress titles may be purchased in bulk for academic, corporate, or promotional use. eBook versions and licenses are also available for most titles. For more information, reference our Print and eBook Bulk Sales web page at http://www.apress.com/bulk-sales.

Any source code or other supplementary material referenced by the author in this book is available to readers on GitHub via the book's product page, located at www.apress.com/978-1-4842-5515-5. For more detailed information, please visit http://www.apress.com/source-code.

Printed on acid-free paper

This book is dedicated to my parents

Table of Contents

About the Author

Jayant Varma is a Developer, Consultant and author that has over 25 years of experience in developing and delivering applications, of which the last decade was focussed solely on iOS. He has worked on many iOS applications that span indie games to Enterprise level applications used by several users from the App store and via Enterprise builds. He loves to be hands on, being closer to the code and manages teams of iOS developers that work at different Enterprise level organisations in Melbourne, Australia. He has worked with/ made apps for NBN, Telstra, Westpac to name a few. He has written several books related to iOS development on topics like Lua, Swift, Objective-C, Xcode, Bash and now SwiftUI. His early days can be dated back to working with Z80 assembly, dBase, Clipper, FoxPro, Visual Basic and even RPG on AS/400.

He has experience in several domains. His love of code can see him dive deep hands-on into code. He is involved with the community and speaks at meetups and conferences, has worked in 3 major universities in Australia and teaches Swift to budding developers. He has also taught Swift to an Apple Education cohort.

He can be reached on Linked in at `https://www.linkedin.com/in/jayantvarma/`

About the Technical Reviewer

Mehul Mohan is an independent developer and security researcher who likes to work with code and create things with it. He runs codedamn (https://www.youtube.com/codedamn) as the platform to share his work with others, and also runs codedamn.com as an independent developer platform for learning and connecting. He's mostly into JavaScript and its runtimes but is eager to explore other interesting technologies. WWDC19 scholar, SwiftUI video series, and author of two books, you can find him using the handle @mehulmpt almost everywhere.

Acknowledgments

Writing a book is not exactly an easy task and more so when the technology is new and does not have a lot of information available. This has been a challenging journey also given the fact that every fortnight there were changes to the API that broke some of the earlier code or changed the way something was done. This book could be completed due to the support by my family, more so my lovely wife Monica who has supported me pulling late nighters and weekends trying out new features of SwiftUI and making sure that it all works and remains current.

A special thanks to my parents that always believed in me and to that effect this is going to be my 7th published book.

Thanks also to Aaron and Jessica at Apress, reaching out to Aaron for a new book pitch and get this process started was quite easy, he got things organised even while he was travelling and responded between his flights. Thanks to Jessica, who as usual made the process easy and a breeze and for all the quick responses and support at all aspects of the process.

Thanks to the Technical reviewer to go through the text and code and highlight the little changes that were missed and special thanks to the team that made this wonderful framework at Apple.

CHAPTER 1

What Is SwiftUI

In this chapter, we'll review the principles of SwiftUI and why it came into being. You'll see the advantages that it offers over traditional methodologies of development and how easy it is to write UI without having to worry much about it in a much more declarative manner.

The Beginnings

Every year, WWDC is always a source of exciting stuff for developers; everyone waits with baited breath to see what new tech is being introduced by Apple. Historically, WWDC, which is the Developers Conference, has been the forum where numerous new and interesting technologies have been previewed for release in some time. The most current groundbreaking piece of tech released by Apple was in 2014 when Apple released Swift, an alternative to the aging Objective-C. This not only had an easier syntax and was based on modern programming fundamentals but was also open sourced. Five years have passed since then and several books and apps are now created using Swift. This year in 2019, at WWDC, Apple released something that got developers all excited once again, called SwiftUI (Figure 1-1). Though this is still a new technology and at the time of writing the book still in beta, it can have some changes which would only add more functionality to the existing repertoire of SwiftUI.

© Jayant Varma 2019
J. Varma, *SwiftUI for Absolute Beginners*, https://doi.org/10.1007/978-1-4842-5516-2_1

Figure 1-1. *Applications built using SwiftUI on Mac, iOS, and WatchOS*

In a single sentence, the easiest way to describe SwiftUI is a declarative UI. This might still not really answer or help understand what it is all about. An easy way to understand declarative UI is to simply state what you want, like *"I want my eggs hard boiled"* instead of detailing the steps like *"get eggs, put them in a pan filled with water, put this on the flame and wait for 7 minutes."* Its more about focusing on what's important than how to achieve that.

In traditional programming languages, one would generally create an UI element; then set its visual frame; set the colors, background and foreground, and other attributes; and then set it up on the visual hierarchy. With declarative, you only need to specify that you need an element, and these can then be modified using modifiers.

SwiftUI Principles

SwiftUI is built on four principles discussed in the following sections.

Declarative

Traditional development was focused more on how to create elements and how to display them on the screen and then continue to update them as the data changes. With a declarative UI, this moves away from that, instead allowing the developer to focus on what you want to display.

Let's see how this looks currently:

```
let labelText = UILabel(frame: CGRect(x:0, y:0, width:100,
height:100))
labelText.text = "Hello World"
labelText.textColor = UIColor.blue
labelText.backgroundColor = UIColor.red
labelText.font = UIFont(name: "Helvetica", size: 24)
self.view.addSubview(labelText)
```

This simply creates a UILabel and then sets its attributes. This code is specific for iOS as it uses the UILabel which is not available on macOS which uses NSLabel or the watchOS which uses WKInterfaceLabel. Now with SwiftUI, there is a common element that is available on all of iOS, iPadOS, macOS, and watchOS. The same code looks like

```
Text("Hello World")
.color(.blue)
.background(Color.red)
.font(.largeTitle)
```

That brings us up to the next principle:

Automatic

This principle is hinged on the basis that it offers automatic functionality; if you saw the preceding code snippet, there was no mention of spacing, frames, insets, and the like. SwiftUI offers all the out-of-the-box features for free functionality - like Localization; if the code had language strings, then the line above would display the localized version, all without writing extra code, all automatically. Developers can also take advantage of functionality like left-to-right, Dark mode, Dynamic type, and more, all with writing minimal code.

Composition

This is another interesting principle that SwiftUI is based on simply because a UI is nothing but a collection of visual elements that together provide the user an interactive experience. With SwiftUI, Apple makes this much easier to manage, even creating complex views by using containers like VStack or HStack. Composition is nothing but creating newer elements by compositing using other elements.

Consistent

Now when Apple wanted to create an easy-to-use application program interface (API), they made sure that it was easy to use. The biggest problem faced with developers is updating the UI from data models; there can be lags and/or issues that prevent the data from being used in the update cycle and can lead to strange errors or behaviors that are difficult to understand. So, to solve this particular problem with data and UI, the fourth principle is important.

Since the UI is a reflection of the data it represents, it should always be in sync so as to provide a consistent experience. Traditionally, this is the step that is error prone as data can be out of sync and/or updated out of cycle. With SwiftUI, the UI updates automatically as soon as the data changes.

It also caters for a temporary UI state that can be simply declared using the @State property wrapper.

> **Note**   With traditional programming, most developers are used to mutability; with SwiftUI, it is surprising how little mutability is required.

SwiftUI Architecture

The advantages of using SwiftUI are not limited to the preceding points; these are just the tip of the iceberg, mostly because it is not very long ago that SwiftUI was released and like the early versions of Swift, there are a lot of changes to be expected. However, most of the principles would still be useful and available even with the organic changes.

The Swift language is open source and there is an evolution web site where the community discusses and progresses the development. SwiftUI is however not open source and managed only by Apple. It is cross platform on the Apple Ecosystems only and works across all of them, iOS, iPadOS, macOS, tvOS, and watchOS (Figure 1-2).

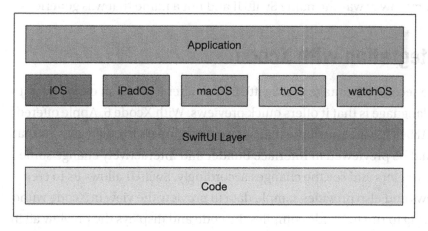

Figure 1-2. *SwiftUI Architecture*

While SwiftUI sits on top of the code and creates the application that displays UI elements, it does not, and please note this (as of now and probably even later), it does not create native elements from the code. So when a developer creates a `text` element, it does not create a `UILabel` or a `NSLabel` or `WKInterfaceLabel`. It is still a `text` element, and in the view debugger, it shows all of the elements, the native ones and the SwiftUI. However, they are displayed separately in their own hierarchies. All of the SwiftUI is hosted in a container called Hosting View; more details of all these are available in subsequent chapters.

Requirements to Use SwiftUI

There are a couple of touch points that use SwiftUI, the first being the newer OS, iOS 13, iPadOS 13, macOS 15, and watchOS 6. From a development perspective, the minimum requirements are Xcode 11 or higher running on macOS 10.15 Catalina or higher, and from a language perspective, it needs the new features added in Swift 5.1. With all of these, it is apparently clear that it is not available with Objective-C; perhaps, the key giveaway was the name SwiftUI and not a name that was generic.

Integration with Xcode

The second advantage that SwiftUI offers after it being an easy declarative UI language is that it offers quick previews. With Xcode 6, Apple offered a `@IBDesignable` attribute that allowed developers to create classes that could be previewed in Interface Builder and interactively change some parameters and see the changes accordingly. SwiftUI allows us to create views and also provides sample data to preview the view in Xcode without having to run it. Xcode compiles the code and displays the preview all in the background as soon as some code is written. If there is a substantial change, then previews are paused, and requesting to resume the preview would compile the code and attempt to preview the UI.

This is a very powerful functionality since it allows developers and designers to quickly create the UI and also preview it with sample data even before it can be shared/deployed to other developers. In fact, there is an entire chapter (Chapter 8) on previews and the functionality that it provides and how it can be harnessed.

SwiftUI Teaser

Before we finish and wrap up this introductory chapter on SwiftUI, here's a teaser of what it looks like in its entirety. It is interesting to see that the preview is inside what looks like the simulator (Figure 1-3).

Figure 1-3. *SwiftUI commands and preview in Xcode*

Summary

In this chapter, we looked at the principles of SwiftUI as to why it came into being and the advantages that it offers over traditional methodologies of development. It also touched upon how easy it is to write UI without having to worry much about it in a much more declarative manner. In the next chapter, we shall look at what makes all of this possible - the magic behind all of the new functionalities in SwiftUI.

CHAPTER 2

Peeking into SwiftUI

In the last chapter, we had a look at SwiftUI and the principles behind SwiftUI. In this chapter, we shall have a look at how SwiftUI can leverage all of these things, what is it that powers SwiftUI. Let's have a peek under the hood on the features that help power them.

Programming languages and techniques have been evolving for over 5 decades. Of the many streams of improvements, one has been to reduce the entry bar for people to start programming - making it easy for all to start development, with a lot of initiatives like the Hour of Code, Girls Who Code, Code Like a Girl, and many more about making development inclusive and accessible to many. Those that know about the programming language used for Apple products, Objective-C was a variant of Smalltalk that was created in the 1970s. This was a very powerful, dynamic programming language, but it was still a language that did not allow all to get on board; it kept a large number of developers away. In 2014, Apple released Swift, a language that was inspired from a lot of modern languages and as a fledgling language began incorporating a lot of features that made it quite flexible and extensive. It was open sourced, and the evolution of the language was managed chiefly by Apple but influenced by open discussion by the community.

Despite the popularity of Swift, there were newer issues that were the bane of a modern developer. This paved the way for several patterns and frameworks to rear their head, like *ReactNative, React, Model View ViewModel (MVVM), VIPER,* and so on. Some of them worked well

© Jayant Varma 2019
J. Varma, *SwiftUI for Absolute Beginners*, https://doi.org/10.1007/978-1-4842-5516-2_2

natively with other platforms or programming languages, but for the Apple ecosystem, they were an add-on, something that did not work natively with the Apple architecture. Despite this, developers were bagging the *MVC* design pattern as Massive-View-Controller instead of the *Model-View-Controller* that it stands for. Separating the code, the view and the model became the foremost thing with most developers.

Principles Behind SwiftUI

Some waited with the standard Apple MVC holding out of these other design patterns mentioned above, and with the introduction of SwiftUI, developers will surely rejoice and accept this design pattern since it is the official response from Apple on this matter.

There are a lot of things that power SwiftUI; however, some of the main ones that really helped bring SwiftUI to life came with Swift 5.1, and these items are listed as follows:

1.   Opaque Return Types (SE-0244)

2.   Implicit return from single-expression functions (SE-0255)

3.   Function Builders

4.   Property Wrappers (SE-0258)

Opaque Return Types

The first evolution feature is *Opaque Return Types*. From the Swift language guide[1], it describes Opaque Return Types as a function or method with an opaque return type hides its return value's type information. Instead of providing a concrete type as the function's return

---

[1]https://docs.swift.org/swift-book/LanguageGuide/OpaqueTypes.html

type, the return value is described in terms of the protocols it supports. Hiding type information is useful at boundaries between a module and code that calls into the module because the underlying type of the return value can remain private. Unlike returning a value whose type is a protocol type, opaque types preserve type identity – the compiler has access to the type information, but clients of the module don't.

Opaque Return Types are described as the reverse of *Generics*; it helps to abstract the full return type from a function while still retaining the complete details of the generic.

Consider the code

```
func add<T: Numeric>(num1: T, num2:T) -> T {
    return num1 + num2
}
```

Now, when this function is called as

```
let res1 = (num1: 3, num2: 2)
    // return type is Int
let res2 = (num1: 1.3, num2: 2.3)
    // return type is Double
```

The return type is determined by the calling code; the function has no sway over the return type. To use Opaque return Types, we use the keyword some, and the return types from the function have to be of a concrete type.

Take the following example:

```
protocol P{}
extension Int: P{}
extension  String: P{}
func add1() -> some P {
    return "Some Value"
}
let res: P = add1()
```

This returns a concrete type of type String, but from the calling code, we do not know what the return type is; what we know for sure is that it conforms to the protocol P.

The following code returns a String Error when the number is 0; otherwise, it returns the number multiplied by 5. This works fine because both String and Int confirm to the Protocol P, and the expected return value from this function add2 is a value of type P.

```
func add2(num: Int) -> P {
    if num == 0 {
        return "Error"
    }
    return num * 5
}
```

This code would work fine, but if we were to expect an Opaque Return type by adding the keyword **some**, this would not work as there is no concrete return type; it returns a String and an Int in its return paths. Opaque Return Types expect that the value returned on all the return paths of a function should be the same concrete type. So, returning a String and an Int breaks this conformance and hence the error.

```
func add2(num: Int) -> some P {
    if num == 0 {
        return "Error"
    }
    return num * 5
} // Error: No concrete return type
```

If this is not clear and confusing, take some time and go over it a couple of times, read the detailed article on Apple's web site. This is important but not something that will be an impediment to program with Swift or inhibit the ability to use SwiftUI.

Differences Between Opaque Types and Protocol Types

As per the Apple documentation, the differences are summarized as follows, returning an opaque type looks very similar to using a protocol type as the return type of a function, but these two kinds of return type differ in whether they preserve type identity. An opaque type refers to one specific type, although the caller of the function isn't able to see which type; a protocol type can refer to any type that conforms to the protocol. Generally speaking, protocol types give you more flexibility about the underlying types of the values they store, and opaque types let you make stronger guarantees about those underlying types.

Implicit Returns from Single-Expression Functions

Another thing that makes SwiftUI such a breeze is *implicit returns*; in simple words and short, it means that there is no need to add the keyword `return` to return a value from a function that has a single expression. Here's a simple example to demonstrate what single-expression could mean:

```
func add(num1: Int, num2: Int) -> Int {
    num1 + num2
}
```

In the preceding code block, the function takes two Ints and returns the sum of both these Ints. Generally, a function would have had the expression "return num1 + num2," but with implicit returns, just the expression can suffice. This makes for some easier to read and lesser code as there are lesser characters to type. Though this is not new as portions of this were already in use with functional programming in Swift, like

```
let names = persons.map { $0.name }
```

This is also very useful in getters where it can be simply used, though personally I find this a bit confusing at times because it takes time to getting used to it. This feature is part of the SE-0255 on the Swift Evolution[2].

Though there has been much discussion on including braces syntax like available in other languages such as *Scala* or *Kotlin*, at the moment, curly braces are very much required as still it gives rise to interesting one liner code like

```
func square(of x: Int) -> Int { x * x }
```

Function Builders

Another thing that makes SwiftUI magical is *Function Builders*. Though in SwiftUI this has a pivotal role to play in terms of UI. This is still under evolution as of writing this book chapter but has an implementation upon which the chapter is based. This is still under active development.

In simple terms, Function Builders are specially annotated functions used to implicitly build a value from a sequence of components. These components are usually in the form of statements and expressions that together produce a single value piece.

This is based on the "*builder pattern*" design pattern, the goal of which is to separate the construction of a complex object from its representation. To understand this, let's look at this block of code that creates a Cell (we are calling it a Cell not UITableViewCell):

```
let cell = StandardCell()
cell.titleLabel.text = cellData.title
cell.subtitleLabel.text = cellData.subtitle
cell.imageView.image = cellData.image
```

---

[2]https://github.com/apple/swift-evolution/blob/master/proposals/0255-omit-return.md

The same in the builder pattern format could look something like

```
let cell = StandardCell()
    .useTitle(cellData.title)
    .useSubtitle(cellData.subtitle)
    .useImage(cellData.image)
    .build()
```

A similar concept was introduced and used earlier, that is, *Fluent interfaces*. The concept of which was that functions can be chained that work on the same object by simply returning the object itself. In code, it could be represented something like

```
class FluentObjectCell {
    func  useTitle(_ title: String) -> Self {
        self.title.text = title
        return self
    }
    func useSubtitle(_ subtitle: String) -> Self {
        self.subtitle.text = subtitle
        return self
    }
    func useImage(_ image: Image) -> Self {
        self.imageView.image = image
        return self
    }
    func build() {
        // build the cell with all the settings here
    }
}
```

This is not a representation of the best or even the good practice but instead just a representation of Fluent interfaces and builder pattern. An actual implementation might be much better; the takeaway from this preceding code is the fact that when functions return the same object usually denoted by Self, then another function can be applied to the same. Another very simple example that we use is that of the String class:

```
let names = "jayant varma"
    .capitalized
    .split(separator: ",")
```

Domain-Specific Languages

Another advantage of using Function Builders is to create *Domain-Specific Languages* (*DSL*); this is nothing but a custom syntax that is created for a particular domain and helps write the structure in that language. The simplest example that is discussed on the Swift Evolution and discussed online is that of creating a HTML DSL:

So, consider the block of HTML code

```
<body>
  <div>
   <h1>Chapter 1. The Chase</h1>
   <p> There was a man from Nantucket</p>
   <p>Who never ever used a bucket</p>
  </div>
  <div>
    <h1>Chapter 2. The wait</h1>
    <p>For want or need</p>
    <p>definitely not out of greed</p>
  </div>
</body>
```

It is simple, and the following is an example of how HTML is written using a custom DSL:

```
return body ([
    div([
```

```
        h1("Chapter 1. The Chase"),
        p([.text("There was a man from Nantucket)]),
        p(.text("Who never ever used a bucket"))
    ]),
    div([
        h1("Chapter 2. The Wait"),
        p([.text("For want or need")]),
        p([.text("definitely not out of greed")])
    ])
])
```

The HTML block is now looking more like code, compose-able as a series of functions. This still looks like functions and parameters, which can then further be simplified with a Function Builder to make it seamless and look something like

```
div {
    h1 { "Chapter 1. The Chase" }
    p { "There was a man from Nantucket" }
    p { "Who had never ever used a bucket" }
}
```

This now starts to look much better and easier to understand and compose to generate HTML from code. Creating a DSL is not in scope of this chapter or the book, but to understand why SwiftUI function can be easily used, this little introduction is important. More information (detailed) on this can be found at the Swift Evolution site[3].

Currently, this feature is also in development with more functionality to be released in Swift 5.2. This includes functions that help to make this work for SwiftUI like `buildBlock`, `buildEither,` and `buildIf` that are currently present in Swift 5.1 and `buildExpression`, `buildFunction,` `buildDo,` and `buildOptional` to be released in Swift 5.2.

---

[3]https://github.com/apple/swift-evolution/blob/9992cf3c11c2d5e0ea20bee
98657d93902d5b174/proposals/XXXX-function-builders.mdsw

Property Wrappers

The last feature on our list that is helpful to understand and powers SwiftUI is feature (SE-0258) called *Property Wrappers*. This was released at WWDC (with Xcode 11 beta) and still was undergoing revision. Property Wrappers by simple definition are wrappers that help create properties without having to write boiler code template code. This can remove a lot of redundant code. In one way, think of these as blueprints, and you can create new properties that can be assigned these blueprints. One does not have to write all the setters and getters again and again for each property variable. It is as simple as applying an annotation to the variable, and all of the templated code is applied at compile time.

Note   If you have used Java, then the easiest parallel that one can draw to *PropertyWrappers* is annotations. This is the swift version of annotations. With some differences, but similar to annotations.

Let's take the example of a standard property declaration in Swift:

```swift
var _property1 : String
var firstName: String {
    get { return _property1.uppercased() }
    set { _property1 = newValue }
}
var _property2 : String
var lastName: String {
    get { return _property2.uppercased() }
    set { _property2 = newValue }
}
```

Note   At this time, the third review for Property Wrappers has concluded and the code below is representative of the changes.

For the sake of understanding, let's say there were some more properties like address, city, and so on; this block of code for simply declaring the custom properties would span to a lot of lines. Using Property Wrappers, this would look something like

```
@propertyWrapper
struct Capitalised {
    private var value: String

    init(wrappedValue value: String) {
        self.value = value.capitalized
    }

    var wrappedValue: String {
        get { value }
        set { value = newValue.capitalized }
    }
}
```

The block to define a *PropertyWrapper* starts with the @ symbol followed by the name of the *PropertyWrapper,* which in the preceding example is `Capitalized`. If the declaration has an `initializer`, it takes a named parameter of `wrappedValue` to match the property name and requires an internal property called `wrappedValue` that powers the `propertyWrapper`.

Now that we have declared a custom property, we can use that with our structures. Let's create a new structure called User that has the firstName and lastName that need to have the behavior of Capitalized that is listed earlier:

```
struct User {
    @Capitalised
    var firstName:String

    @Capitalised
    var lastName:String
}
```

A property with the required behavior can be declared as simply prefixing the property declaration with the name of the property wrapper. The variable can be declared with or without a value, that is, can be instantiated later.

And lastly after declaring this, let's create a user instance:

```
let user = User(firstName: "jayant", lastName: "varma")
print(user.firstName, user.lastName)
```

The output shows that the firstName and the lastName are both printed in capital letters.

This is the simplest example to show what *PropertyWrappers* do. To summarize, it works on the following basis:

1. For the PropertyWrapper block, declare a struct, and add to it an initializer based on the local properties created and a wrappedValue property.

2. Use this definition in a class, struct, or another enum with a property element that is of the @propertyWrapper annotation.

3. Any additional functions or properties declared and defined in the propertyWrapper are not available from outside.

If these things are catered for, then it is all set to work.

Additional parameters can be added to the `initializer,` and these are then used when annotating the variable with the `propertyWrapper`. Since this is new, currently, there is no functionality to debug or throw and handle errors.

Common Property Wrappers that are available and would be used often while programming with SwiftUI are wrappers such as `@State`, `@BindableObject`, `@EnvironmentObject`, these are used quite commonly.

Summary

In this chapter, we looked at some of the interesting features that are part of Swift and how they help fuel the functionality that is required for SwiftUI. One thing to note is that Swift is open source whereas SwiftUI is not open source. Secondly, it is still under beta and wants developer feedback to help complete/better this product.

In the next chapter, we shall start looking at the UI elements and understand the differences and similarities between them and their native counterparts that are exclusive to a platform.

CHAPTER 3

Views and Controls

In the last chapter, we looked at what makes SwiftUI tick, the features that make the magic happen. However, that was a bit dry, mostly consisting of theory. The big thing in capitals that makes up and is part of SwiftUI is UI – that which is visual. So, in this chapter, we shall look at the various UI elements and their native UIKit counterparts. This could also function as a ready reckoner to help choose the appropriate element as required.

Everything Is a View

In SwiftUI, almost everything is a view, and this is different from the traditional View, the UI element that we are used to with Objective-C and Swift native UIKit object. Another thing to note is that the object is called View, unlike UIView for iOS or NSView for MacOS. This view is not a struct or a class as it used to be earlier, it is actually a Protocol. The functionality of *Opaque Returns* allows swift to use the "some" keyword as a return parameter in functions; for more details, please refer back to Chapter 2. Another thing to note is that almost all objects conform to the View protocol and have an associated type variable called body, which is in turn again a View. In some objects like Color, this is set to Never which is the equivalent of nil but indicates that the function will not return. It is easy to mistake it for Void as Void returns nothing but a Never function does not return at all.

Modifiers

While this chapter would go through the various UI elements that SwiftUI offers, there is another layer that works with these elements called *modifiers* that work on the elements and provide a customized element. In simpler words, there is a text label, but it may have a background color, or a text color, font size, and so on. These are all set using modifiers on the UI elements. The modifiers follow the declaration and are like a function of that object. Consider the code

```
Text("Hello World")
```

This simply creates a text label in the middle of the screen that displays the text value "**Hello World**." Now this can be made to look larger using the Title style of the font as

```
Text("Hello World")
    .font(.title)
```

And that's that. Modifiers can also be chained to provide a series of customizations, like the same code can also contain a background color, a text color to look like

```
Text("Hello World")
    .font(.title)
    .background(Color.blue)
    .foregroundColor(Color.white)
```

Note   Further to this in the chapter, the elements available in SwiftUI are listed, and the equivalent elements available for iOS, MacOS, or WatchOS are mentioned. The primary comparison is mainly with iOS. While most commonly used SwiftUI elements would work on iOS, MacOS, and WatchOS, the reference to iOS means UIKit and MacOS means AppKit and so on.

Getting Started

XCode11 now has a new feature called *previews*; we shall talk about this in detail in Chapter 8. For now, it is important to know that while we are designing or writing the code, the previews can display and update the layout from code onto the screen. For this, all we need to do is start a new iOS single view project, and all of the code that we will write or modify for this chapter will be in the ContentView.swift file.

The Generic View

The nomenclature of using a generic object name also helps to decouple the objects from a platform, so it is no longer UIView or NSView but simply a View, or no longer UIColor or NSColor but simply Color.

Consider the following code snippet:

```
import SwiftUI
struct ContentView: View {
    let name: String = "Unknown"
    var body: some View {
        return Text("Hello \(name)")
    }
}
```

In this code block, we can see that it defines a struct called ContentView that conforms to the protocol View. This is the smallest unit of an object that can be displayed on screen or be part of a viewable object hierarchy on screen.

The definition has a constant called name, which could be set when the struct is initialized, and it has a computed property called body which will return something that is of type View. In this case, we return a Text type with the text Hello, and the value held in the variable name appended to it.

This is our first element of this chapter, a container called View, which is a UI element on screen. It can contain other views to build a composite view leading to a complex visual layout. This is the equivalent of a UIViewController in iOS.

Note   We can remove the return keyword from the preceding code. Refer to the last chapter for more on this.

Text

The simplest and easiest way to display text on the device/screen is by using a Label. With iOS, we are used to using an UILabel and then setting its text property to the string that we want displayed:

```
let label = UILabel()
label.text = "Testing"
```

With SwiftUI, it is simply as simple as declaring a Text tag as

```
Text("Hello SwiftUI")
```

It is initialized with the text "Hello SwiftUI".

Images

Another most used class in developing the UI is the ImageView. It allows for loading an image from the device or from the system. With iOS, the way is to instantiate an UIImageView and then set the image property with a UIImage that is instantiated with the name of the resource file like

```
let imageView = UIImageView()
let image = UIImage(named:"avatar.png")
imageView.image = image
```

This will still not display anything because it needs the image to be present and secondly the ImageView needs to be given a size and needs to be added to the ViewController's subviews. Consider the following code in SwiftUI:

```
Image("avatar")
```

That is all it takes to display an image on the screen. The only issue is that this image is present in the Assets, not just the bundle. To load an image from the bundle, we have to load it as an UIImage and then provide that to the Image initializer as in the following code:

```
guard let image = UIImage(named: "avatar.jpg") else {
    fatalError("Unable to load the image")
}
Image(uiImage: image)
```

In addition to this, SwiftUI has added a font called SF Symbols; it is a series of symbols that can be used as images with a simple parameter of systemName while initializing the image like

```
Image(systemName:"clock")
```

This preceding code will display the clock icon from the symbols. Apple has an app called SF Symbols that lists out all of the symbols available along with the name of the symbols. The advantage of this is that the images match the text sizes so that they integrate and provide a better UI experience. These can be modified with the color and even the weight; it has 9 weights available right from Ultralight to Heavy Black.

Buttons [Button]

Creating buttons in SwiftUI is as simple as using the Button element. This is much simpler than creating a UIButton and then assigning the Title to display the text on the button. Consider the code

```
let button = UIButton()
button.setTitle("Click me", for: .normal)
```

In the preceding code, the dimensions are not as yet set and nor have the actions to take when the button is tapped. The same with SwiftUI looks like

```
Button (
    action: {
        // handle the tap
    },
    label: {Text("Click Me")}
)
```

This can also be expressed in a shorter simpler manner such as

```
Button("Click Me") {
    //handle the tap
}
```

Toggle [icon]

When faced with binary decision or choices, we can use a switch called Toggle in SwiftUI. This displays the switch in either of the states, On or Off as it can toggle between the two. The iOS equivalent is a UISwitch. The simplest way to use a Toggle in SwiftUI is as follows, where we need to pass it a binding @State variable:

```
Toggle(isOn: $binding) {
    Text("Using High Resolution")
}
```

However, there is one little quirk that we will look into in detail in the next chapter, but for now, we shall use it for illustrative purposes only. It is a property wrapper called State. It is used to handle a mutable value and is declared in the struct but before the computed property as

```
@State var isHiRes = false
```

And then it is used as

```
Toggle(isOn: $isHiRes) {
    Text("Using High Resolution")
}
```

It can also be used to conditionally display elements on the screen as in

```
if isHiRes {
    Text("Using 8K resolution")
}
```

Or better still to not have SwiftUI complain about the missing return keyword, we could write the same as follows:

```
Text(isHiRes ? "Using 8K resolution", "")
```

TextField

In the list of other controls, a developer would use commonly a TextField; it is the easiest way to get textual input from the user. With iOS or MacOS, it is slightly more involved where it needs to set a delegate that handles the keypresses and the text change. Once again, with SwiftUI, it is quite simple and easy, no need for any delegates and extra code setup. However, since the TextField needs to be bound to a variable that holds the text, which is entered, it needs to be backed by a State variable like we used in the Toggle example. Consider the following code:

```
@State var name = "Unknown"
```

And then

```
TextField("placeholder", $name) {}
```

This will display a TextField on the screen, and when it is changed, the value is automatically set in the name variable. It can be chained to achieve something like

```
Text("Hello \(name)")
TextField("Enter Your name here", $name) {}
```

And as the user changes the text in the text field, the value of the text changes automatically. No code is required to update the display – that's the beauty of binding.

If there is a need to enter passwords or not display the text in the TextField, there is no modifier that simply creates the TextField into a secure password TextField. Instead, there is an alternative element called SecureField that can be used as

```
@State var password = ""
SecureField($password){}
```

Now, it allows the entry of password in the text field.

In either case, if it is difficult to see the TextField as the background is white and there are no borders, the borders can be set on the TextField or the SecureField showing its outline with setting the textFieldStyle as roundedBorder:

```
TextField("", $name){}
    .textFieldStyle(.roundedBorder)
```

Slider

Another element that is commonly used to provide a range for the user to select from is the Slider. It has a track that one can use to slide it across to select a value. (It is called an UISlider on iOS) and then add the action to process the changes. With SwiftUI, it is much simpler, and once again, it requires a state to back the slider value:

```
@State var degrees = 0.0
```

And then construct a Slider that uses this as a backing variable:

```
Slider(value: $degrees, from: -99.0, through: 99.0, by: 0.1)
Text("\(degrees)C is \(Int(degrees * 9/5 + 32))F")
```

And voila in two lines, we have a temperature convertor.

Stepper

An alternative UI element is a stepper control, which like these controls also requires a backing variable. The iOS equivalent for this is UIStepper. Using a stepper is quite simple and can be used as

```
@State var steps = 0
Stepper("Steps \(steps)", value: $steps, in: 0...10)
```

And that's all there is to use a stepper.

Segmented Control

There is an UI overhaul on the segmented Control in iOS13, and it looks much better. This has gone through a few changes; Now, it is part of the PickerView and one of the PickerStyles available. This control is common in some UIs. In iOS, a Segmented Control is created by using a `UISegmentedControl` and then by adding the values to display in each segment. This is used for changing interfaces or simply to provide a fixed choice between some options. Consider the code

```
@State var gameMode = 0
```

And then in the computed Property of body, the code

```
Picker("GameMode", selection: $gameMode, content: {
    ForEach(0..<modes.count) { index in
        Text(self.modes[index])
        .tag(index)
    }
})
```

The modes also need to be declared which we can specify easily as

```
var modes = ["Easy", "Difficult", "Insane"]
```

and we have a game difficulty selector without doing much. The value is stored in the binding variable gameMode and can be used as required. Parts of the UI could be displayed or hidden depending on the value.

Picker ▤

The `UIPickerView` is a critical UI element that is not as common as the other elements from the standard UIKit controls in iOS, and this is mainly seen in Mobile Safari during selecting a drop down. This control requires a backing value to store the result and content to display in the picker view:

```
@State var college = 0
var unis = ["JCU", "CQU", "QUT", "UQ", "Monash", "RMIT"]
```

```
Picker(selection: $college, content:{
    ForEach(0..<unis.count) { uni in
        Text(self.unis[uni])
        .tag(uni)
    }
})
```

This would bring up the picker wheel that can be scrolled to select a value. There is an alternative look and feel for the PickerView; when it is embedded in a form element, it changes its look entirely. It displays a table view with a value which when clicked would navigate to a list of values and allow selection from one of those values or the user could simply click back to return the default selected value.

DatePicker 🖵

Another UI Element not commonly used but similar to the PickerView is the DatePicker or the UIDatePickerView in iOS. This allows the user to select a date using a PickerView. The elements that can be selected are set using the date components parameter which are normally .date and .hourAndMinute. The .date simply displays the month, day, and year to select from, while .hourAndMinute displays the hour, minute, and AM/PM indicator. Combining both of these parameters displays the day in dayOfTheWeek, month, and day as one cog of the wheel and the time as the other three with hour, minute, and AM/PM indicator. Similar to the PickerView, the look and feel of this control changes when embedded in a form. It is similar in looks with the PickerView; however, when the element is tapped to select, instead of navigating to a new screen, it drops down the DatePicker to select from, and tapping on the element again

33

dismisses the drop down. The cherry on the icing in this case is that when the drop down starts to show, it does not overlap the elements underneath; instead, it scrolls them out of the way:

```
@State var whensTheDate = Date()
DatePicker("When is the big day?",
    selection: $whensTheDate,
    in: Date()...,
    displayedComponents: [.date, .hourAndMinute])
```

The dateRange is used to limit the date values, and this can be a closed range, that is, fixed between two date/time values, or a minimumDate, which means starting from a particular date and into the infinite future (which is quite difficult as the date picker does not offer a year cog to select, so it will be like slots machine, spinning the wheel quite a few times to get to the previous or next year). The other option is a maximumDate which means a date up until the provided date. The DatePicker displays dates and times beyond the maximum date displayed, but the wheel scrolls back to the maximum on selection.

The preceding example shows the minimumDate, that is, a date/time in the future from now. The maximumDate can be set by simply using the ...Date() instead. However, this is fine for an example to understand how this works; in a production-ready application setting, a value like this might not be such a good idea.

NavigationView

Another commonly used element that is not really thought of as an element is the NavigationView or referred to as the UINavigationController in iOS. We cannot push any new view controllers onto the navigation stack if the UINavigationController was not defined, and then when the viewController is pushed onto the stack, it displays the back button and provides the functionality to pop the viewController off the stack all for free, that is, without having to write any code for it. With SwiftUI, the NavigationView is slightly more than just a UINavigationController; it is also the UINavigationBar and also the UINavigationBarItem, that is, all of the Navigation related items are now encapsulated into the NavigationView element.

The simplest way to use a NavigationView is by declaring it first and then adding the components within the block; consider the code

```
NavigationView {
    NavigationLink("Click to Master",
        destination: Text("You have mastered this domain"))
        .navigationBarTitle("Domain Mastered")
}
```

This code would display a button with the text Click to Master, and upon tapping the same, it would push a new viewController with the title Domain Mastered. If we wrap this in a navigationView, then it also presents the back button to get back to the main screen.

NavigationLink

In the preceding code, we also saw another Navigation-related item called NavigationLink; there is no equivalent of this in iOS. The closest equivalent can be found with *HTML*, as A tag, which allows for hyperlink and clicking on which would present another page or position in the page. However, when the destination is presented, it is not pushed onto the navigation stack; it is displayed as a dismissible sheet that can be flicked down to dismiss. The code sample can be seen in the preceding example.

NavigationBarItems

The NavigationView comprises the TitleBar, and it could have buttons on the left and on the right. These buttons can be added using the .navigationBarItems modifier of the NavigationView element. The iOS equivalent of this is UIBarButtonItem. It is quite easy to use, and the two buttons left and right are referred to as leading and trailing views in SwiftUI.

Since the leading and trailing are views, this can be anything, Text, Image, or Button; however, it makes most sense to have a Button in the interface so that it is interactive and can provide some activity when tapped, like change to edit mode, provide a set of options, and so on:

```
NavigationView {
    List { Text("Hello World")}
    .navigationBarItems(trailing:
        Button("Click me") {
            //
        })
    .navigationBarTitle(Text("Settings"))
}
```

This provides a layout that has a button on the top right corner, a large title bar with the text Settings, and a table view with a single item Hello World. Earlier, we saw how to use a button; the same can be applied to provide this button with functionality.

TabView

When creating a complex interface, there might come the need to have multiple viewControllers; while some of the elements mentioned earlier can help group or separate UI elements, one common way is to have a tabbed view layout. The equivalent for this in iOS is called a UITabBarController. It is quite simple; it has a number of tabs, and each tab has a viewController attached to it, so when the tab is changed, the viewController for that tab is displayed.

With SwiftUI, this can be created by using the declaration TabView, and it requires three things, it needs a View to display for that tab, it needs a tag that is unique as this is what could be bound to a backing variable to get the currently selected tab, and the last thing is a .tabItem; this is the view that shows the tab at the bottom of the TabView:

```
TabView{
    Text("First Controller View")
    Text("Second Controller View")
}
```

This works, but it only displays the text First Controller View on screen; there is no way to select the second controller or switch the tab. That is because we have not as yet created the tabItems:

```
TabView{
    Text("First Controller View")
        .tabItem({Text("first")})
    Text("Second Controller View")
        .tabItem({Text("second")})
}
```

Now, the screen displays the text at the bottom so that the tabs can be changed; however, on tapping the second tab, it does not display anything. That is because we have not yet provided it a tag, which we can by simply using the .tag modifier as

```
TabView{
    Text("First Controller View")
        .tabItem({Text("first")})
        .tag(0)
```

```
        Text("Second Controller View")
            .tabItem({Text("second"})
            .tag(1)
    }
```

The tabs now work fine, but it does not still look professional and elegant, that is because they are missing an image. That can be easily rectified by adding an Image view along with the Text view in the .tabItem as

```
    TabView{
        Text("First Controller View")
            .tabItem({
                Image(systemName:"1.circle.filled")
                Text("first")
            })
            .tag(0)
        Text("Second Controller View")
            .tabItem({
                Image(systemName:"2.circle.filled")
                Text("second")
            })
            .tag(1)
    }
```

Stacks

So far, we have looked at the common elements that are used for layouts in an UI. Apple released UIStackView as a way to provide an alternative for UI layouts; this was used with iOS quite popularly to house a rather complex interface quite easily. With SwiftUI, this could not be disregarded, and it is available in a couple of forms, namely, Horizontal Stack (HStack), Vertical

Stack (VStack), and Aligning on both Axis (ZStack). The Stacks are also a way to group by using an alternative to the element Group and create a complex layout; Stacks can be nested inside of other stacks.

Note Something that is not apparent is that there can be up to 10 views passed to a view builder function, which is a limitation based off the way the source code is, to be able to add more elements than just 10. The 10 is not a magic number but comes from the function called ViewBuilder that has the buildBlock function defined as

```
public static func buildBlock<C0, C1, C2, C3, C4,
C5, C6, C7, C8, C9>(_ c0: C0, _ c1: C1, _ c2: C2,
_ c3: C3 ...) -> TupleView<(C0, C1, ... C9)> where
C0: View, C1: View ... C9: View
```

The buildBlock is defined for taking 1 to 10 parameters similar to the 10 parameter version illustrated earlier.

HStack

The first of the three stacking methodologies is HStack; this aligns the child elements horizontally, side by side on the X axis (from left to right). The closest equivalent to HStack in iOS is UIStackView with the axis set to horizontal:

```
HStack {
    Text("Hello")
    Text("World")
}
```

This would result in the text Hello World displayed side by side. This is useful for creating a layout that has say an image and text inline like

```
HStack{
    Image(systemName:"signature")
    Text("Sign Here")
}
```

This can be used for tableview cells, buttons, and so on. that require the image and text to be aligned in the same horizontal axis.

VStack

The second Stacking methodology is using VStack; this aligns the elements vertically, one below the other on the Y axis (from Top to bottom). The closest equivalent to VStack in iOS is UIStackView with the axis set to vertical:

```
VStack {
    Text("Hello")
    Text("World")
}
```

This would result in the text Hello and World displayed one below the other. This is also used for complex layouts and compositing layouts as we shall see further in the chapter.

ZStack

There is no equivalent for this in iOS. This is specifically created for SwiftUI to allow aligning the elements in respect to each other in the Z-axis, actually stacked on top of each other:

```
ZStack {
    Text("Hello")
    Text("World")
}
```

This will result in both the elements overlaid on top of the other. This is good for compositing images and views with absolute positions which can be achieved by using the .offset modifier as

```
ZStack {
    Text("Hello")
    Text("World")
        .offset(x: 0, y: 20)
}
```

And now, it seems that it is as if arranged in a VStack.

These Stack elements can also be initialized with initializer values that do away with the need of modifier values and are applied to all of the children. These take three parameters, namely, alignment, spacing, and content. So far, we have been providing the content directly using the curly braces. The alignment parameter aligns the child elements using leading, trailing, or center, and the spacing is the spacing between the children:

```
VStack(alignment: .leading, spacing: 20) {
    Text("Hello")
    Text("World")
}
```

ScrollView

When the content becomes larger than the screen can display, we are so used to simply swiping at the screen to make it scroll and see the rest of the content. ScrollView is quite important in creating Layout and UIs. In fact,

41

majority of the times, scrolling is provided by the system, and we are not even aware that there is a `Scrollview`. The only time it actually reminds us of its presence is when we have to create it manually. The iOS equivalent is UIScrollView and requires a lot of settings to be made to ensure that the content scrolls. With SwiftUI, it is quite simple and is declared as

```
ScrollView {
    Text("Hello")
    Text("World")
}
```

The content is now scrollable; if we swipe the screen up or down, the content moves with the swipe. Note that it does not scroll horizontally, just vertically.

This can be changed by simply initializing the ScrollView with the appropriate axis and settings to show the scroll indicators as

```
ScrollView([.horizontal, .vertical], showIndicators: true) {

    Text("Hello")
    Text("World")
}
```

Decorators

There are some other elements that have no direct correlation or equivalence in the UI kits used in either iOS, MacOS, or WatchOS. However, these added to SwiftUI provide amazing composite layouts.

Spacer

Spacer is a simple flexible space that can be applied on the axis of the stack layout. So, in a HStack, it is horizontal space, and on VStack, it is a vertical space. If this is not contained in a stack, then it is applied on both axes.

This is used in complex layouts to spread or space elements to fill the space available. It can be used simply as itself:

```
Spacer()
```

In our example of VStack, the text for Hello and World are in the center of the screen; if we apply a Spacer in the middle, it will push the Hello to the top and World to the bottom filling up the center:

```
VStack {
    Text("Hello")
    Spacer()
    Text("World")
}
```

Divider

Another decorator element that is used for complex layouts is the Divider; it is the equivalent of a line used to separate content. The closest equivalent that it reminds me of is that of the HR element (Horizontal Rule) from HTML. However, this can draw a divider on either X or Y axis. Its use is also quite simple:

```
HStack {
    Text("Hello")
    Divider()
    Text("World")
}
```

Using Stacks and Dividers can also yield some very interesting results, like creating grids or rulers as in the following code:

```
ZStack {
    VStack {
```

```
            ForEach(-2..<3) { index in
                Divider()
                .offset(x: 0, y: CGFloat(index * 20))
            }
        }
    }
    HStack {
        ForEach(-2..<3) { index in
            Divider()
            .offset(x: CGFloat(index * 20), y: 0)
        }
    }
}
```

Alert

We are used to being notified on the mobile or the desktop whenever something happens, and the alertBox appears with the message and a button to dismiss it. With iOS, the API has changed from an AlertBox to an AlertViewController, but with SwiftUI, it is simpler and yet a bit complex.

Since alerts are displayed and can be dismissed, it gets complex. With the state binding, alerts can be thought of as something that can be displayed on a particular state. So, when the alert is dismissed, the state is set to false, so displaying an alert is as simple as setting the state to true. If that did not make a lot of sense, look at the following code:

```
@State var showAlert = false
Button("Show Alert") {
    self.showAlert = true
}.alert(isPresented: $showAlert) {
    Alert(title: Text("Alert Box"),
```

```
         message: Text("This is our first Alert Message"),
         dismissButton: .default(Text("OK"))
    )
 }
```

The code displays the alert when the value of showAlert is true, and when the alert is dismissed, the value of showAlert is set to false. Therefore, to show the alert again, the value of showAlert needs to be set to true. This is what the code does when the button is pressed, and the alert is displayed automatically. Alternatively, the line self.showAlert = true can be set to self.showAlert.toggle().

Note   There is a new addition in Swift for Boolean; it is a method called toggle; this toggles the value held in the Boolean. So, if it is true, it is set to false, and if it is false, it is set to true.

List

Majority of the user interfaces on a mobile device can be represented via table views, a simple and elegant form of displaying data. The advantage of using TableViews is that it adds scrolling and other functionalities for free, that is, none of that has to be explicitly managed by the developer. By far, a majority of iOS applications are made up of UITableView with standard or custom Cells. With MacOS applications, it is slightly more complicated and tedious trying to set up the UI using some form of a TableView like an OutlineView or a Hierarchicy view.

The closest equivalent in SwiftUI is simply called List, and the cells that make up the cells are simply composite views that are used together in place of a cell.

45

Consider the code

```
List {
    Text("One")
    Text("Two")
    Text("Three")
}
```

This creates a simple table on screen that can be scrolled. A longer table can be created by adding more elements to the list as in the following code:

```
List(0..<50) { item in
    Text("Item # \(item)")
}
```

That will create a table with 50 items that can be scrolled.

Creating a Custom Cell

As mentioned earlier, a custom cell is nothing but a composite view which would take the place of Text("Item # \(item)") in the preceding code. We have so far seen that views can be grouped, or composite views can be made by using Stacks. A cell row can be created with a combination of HStack and VStack as required:

```
List(0..<5) { item in
    HStack{
        Image(systemName: "person")
        Text("User number \(item)")
    }
}
```

This can further be made into a proper UI layout by adding a NavigationView, a Title, and a NavigationLink. With just a couple of lines of code, we have a simple static table ready:

```
NavigationView {
    List(0..<5) { item in
        NavigationLink(destination : Text("User \(item)")){
            HStack {
                Image(systemName: "person")
                Text("User numer \(item)")
            }
        }.navigationBarTitle(Text("Users"))
    }
}
```

The standard table view is that of a plain table, with the style UITableView.Style.plain; this displays the table as a series of rows, and this can also be changed to use the UITableView.Style.grouped style which looks more like the Settings table that has groupings as we will do in the next section:

```
NavigationView {
  List {
    Section(header: Text("Section One")) {
      ForEach(0..<3) { index in
        NavigationLink(destination: Text("Item \(index)")){
          Text("Section item \(index)")
        }
      }
    }
```

```
        Section(header: Text("Section Two")) {
          ForEach(50..<55) { index in
            NavigationLink(destination: Text("Area \(index)")){
              Text("Restricted Area \(index)")
            }
          }
        }
      }.navigationBarTitle(Text("Applications"))
  }
```

Sections

This brings us to another feature of tables, namely, sections. Sections are a simple way to create groupings and separating the items in the List. The sections do not need to, but can, have a header and a footer. Since these are views, they can be anything as simple as a Text element or a composite view consisting of several views:

```
Section(header: Text("Header"),
        footer: Text("this is a footer")) {
    Text("This is the sections' contents")
}
```

This will create a table view that has the header with the Text Header with the text Header and a footer with the text this is a footer. It can also house images by simply adding a HStack and an Image as

```
List {
Section(header: HStack {
    Image(systemName: "person.fill")
    Text("Corporate Users")
    }) {
        ForEach(0..<3) { index in
```

```
        HStack {
            Image(systemName: "person")
            Text("User id : \(index)")
        }
    }
  }
}
```

We can change this table view list which is in plain format to be in a grouped format by simply using the `.listStyle` modifier and pass it the style of `GroupedListStyle` as

```
.listStyle(GroupedListStyle())
```

Summary

This was a largish chapter, but that is also because there are so many visual elements that exist; we shall explore the other elements in further chapters. In this chapter, we have looked at the various elements and their equivalent that exist in UIKit and seen how it takes lesser lines of code to achieve some very complex functionality that ordinarily took several lines of code. In the next chapter, we shall look at *States* and *Data Flow* and explore more about how they work and what purpose they serve.

CHAPTER 4

Data and Combine

In the last chapter, we covered a lot of UI elements and had a look at how they work. We shall explore more UI elements in the chapters as we go forward; however, there were some interesting things, namely, the @State annotation that we used to store values. In this chapter, we shall explore this and the related information on how it all works and makes this possible.

Data

While creating SwiftUI, the engineers at Apple looked at a lot of things that could do with improvements, and many of the techniques and technology released at WWDC make development easier, readable, and manageable.

Data was the first thing that Apple looked at, and while building SwiftUI from the ground up, they tried to solve the complexity of UI Development, and it ensures that Data is a first-class citizen. In the context of programming, it is defined as *"An entity which supports all the operations generally available to other entities. These operations typically include being passed as an argument, returned from a function, modified, and assigned to a variable."*

© Jayant Varma 2019
J. Varma, *SwiftUI for Absolute Beginners*, https://doi.org/10.1007/978-1-4842-5516-2_4

What Is Data

Data is the information that drives the UI, and it comes in various forms, like in @State that holds the state of the toggle or data as in the Data Model which drives the UI.

There are two driving principles for Data that Apple worked on when creating SwiftUI and specifically in terms of SwiftUI.

Every time a piece of data is read in view, *a dependency is created for that view*. It is called a dependency because it is paramount that every time this information changes, the view needs to reflect those changes. This is quite simple and trivial, but as the applications become larger, this can become quite complex.

Every piece of data read into the view hierarchy is *the source of truth*; this data is stored in the view hierarchy. There can be instances where there might be duplicated sources of truth, and this can lead to bugs and UI artifacts that lead to bad user experience. So, a lot of care has to be taken to ensure that they are in sync, and yet it is easy to make a mistake. Instead of having this, the suggestion is to move the stored data in a common ancestor and let the children have a reference to it. This will thereby allow for a single *source of truth*.

Mutating Variables

With Swift, we are aware that all structs are value types and classes are reference types. This is something that we need to keep in mind. The second thing is that value types are generally immutable. With that in mind, let us look at this code that is simple Swift code using a struct and a single variable called seatNumber that can be modified using the bookSeat function:

```
struct Seat {
    var seatNumber: Int
```

```
func bookSeat(seatNumber: Int) {
    self.seatNumber = seatNumber
    }
}
```

At the face of it, the code seems fine, and we can compile it. However, if we refer back to the start of this section, this is a struct, and we agreed that structs are immutable. The compiler will complain that that code cannot be compiled because it cannot assign to the property as the struct is immutable. This is easy and can be fixed; we can simply add the keyword mutating in front of the function and all good.

Let's modify this a little and say that instead of a seat number this is a struct that holds the information about the seat instead as

```
struct Seat {
    private var booked = false

    var toggleBooking: Bool {
        return self.booking.toggle()
    }
}
```

We have the complier complaining again, and this time around, we cannot simply prefix the mutating keyword to the computed property.

@State

Apple created a *Property Wrapper* called @State to address this very issue. We had a look at Property Wrappers in detail in the last chapter, and it helps by encapsulating the value to allow modifying it from an immutable struct. This and a couple of other Property Wrappers are important to make SwiftUI efficient and magical.

So, adding the @State before the booked variable will appease the compiler, but please note that it will not work because a @State *PropertyWapper* binds an UI element with a variable.

So, let's create a new file of type SwiftUI called Seat:

```
struct Seat: View {
    @State private var booked = false

    var body: some View {
        Text("Seat is \(booked ? "Booked" : "Available" )")
    }

    var toggleBooking: Bool {
        return self.booked.toggle()
    }
}
```

The @State *is not the value but provides the means to reading and mutating the value.* SwiftUI manages the storage of any property, and when the state value changes, the view invalidates its appearance and recomputes its body. In other words, it tells SwiftUI that the @State variable is a value that can change at some point and that the view is dependent on this value, so whenever the value changes, the view must be updated with the new value.

Let's make it an interactive SwiftUI component by adding a button to change the seat booked state:

```
var body: some View {
    VStack {
        Text("Seat is \(booked ? "Booked" : "Available" )")
        Button(booked ? "Release" : "Book") {
            self.booked.toggle()
        }
    }
}
```

This view encapsulates its own booked state, and whenever the state changes, it updates the text to Release or Book as per the case. The text displays the status as Booked or Available as can be seen in Figure 4-1.

Seat is Available
Book

Figure 4-1. *The view displaying the Text and the button*

The beauty of SwiftUI and these bindings allow for creating UI easily. We can very simply substitute the text for a graphic and set the color accordingly as can be seen in Figure 4-2:

```
var body: some View {
  VStack {
    HStack {
      Text("Seat Status : ")
      Image(systemName: booked ? "xmark" : "checkmark")
        .foregroundColor(booked ? .red : .green)
    }. font(.largeTitle)
    Button(booked ? "Release" : "Book") {
      self.booked.toggle()
    }
  }
}
```

Figure 4-2. *The view with graphic symbol and color*

View Updates

When a state variable changes, the state knows the view that is managing the state and sends a message to this view to update itself and its children. All of the views and subviews are updated, efficiently because the runtime knows which views to update based on which views have changed or are affected with that state change. The framework does all of this work for us. According to Apple, **every @State is a source of truth** and **the views are a function of state**, not a sequence of events.

Traditionally, events occur, and based on these events, we write the code to mutate the view, that is, add or remove a view or a subview, and change the color or other attributes. With SwiftUI, everything hinges upon the state, and it is the state that acts as the source of truth that drives the view when it mutates or changes. With the declarative syntax of SwiftUI, the states can be used to describe the view layout easily and manage the complexities of UI layout. With the flow seen in Figure 4-3, the flow of data is unidirectional, that is, it flows in one direction only. The state is the single point where all changes are managed. This makes the whole process easy to manage as the flow is predictable and easy to understand.

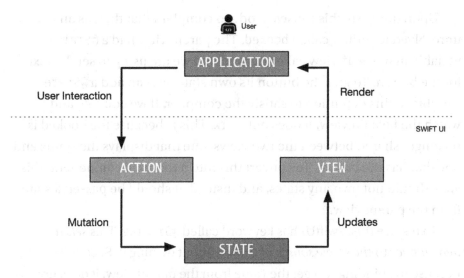

Figure 4-3. *SwiftUI behind the scenes interaction*

Abstracting a View

Now that we understand the state and how it all ties in with the UI updates, let's look at making our button better. How about we give it an icon and as a good practice even abstract it out as its own view. With Xcode 11, we can simply select the element and Command (⌘) and click on the element and select Extract View; this extracts the element and creates a new View definition called ExtractedView for it:

```
struct ExtractedView: View {
    var body: some View {
        Button(booked ? "Release" : "Book") {
            self.booked.toggle()
        }
    }
}
```

Upon doing so, this causes Xcode to complain that there is an unresolved identifier called booked. The parent view had a @State variable in the Seat view called booked that we are using to set the text for the button. To give the button its own state, we can add a @State variable in this definition to satisfy the compiler. If we compile and watch the Live Preview, it does not work. This is because the booked is no longer shared between the two views, one that displays the status and one that has the button. To convert this into a reusable component, this view should not own any states, and instead, it should be passed a state from the parent view.

To resolve this, SwiftUI has keyword called @Binding. This *sets a dependency* to *the single source of truth* without owning it. Secondly, because the binding will get the value from the parent view, it does not require a default value assigned to it:

```
struct ExtractedView: View {
    @Binding var booked: Bool
    var body: some View {
        Button(booked ? "Release" : "Book") {
            self.booked.toggle()
        }
    }
}
```

First, let us rename this function to something meaningful. We can right-click on the function and select *Rename* from the context menu and rename this to, say, BookingButton.

The compiler will still give an error because it needs the initializer for BookingButton. We can pass it the value to booked from the parent view (Seat) as

```
BookingButton(booked: $booked)
```

There is something interesting here; the value passed to the initializer has a **$** prefix. This is new in SwiftUI, and it is a way to tell the runtime that this value should be accessible via the binding for reading and mutating.

The BookingButton does not have a copy of the booked variable; it refers to the Seat view's copy – the source of truth in this case. If we create a couple of buttons, they will all refer to the same variable. We can try by adding the same line a couple of times:

```
BookingButton(booked: $booked)
BookingButton(booked: $booked)
BookingButton(booked: $booked)
```

Though this is not very useful, we can see that the BookingButton is now a reusable component that can mutate the booked state for any view that provides the information, and all of these instances can by synched with the same information. The booked value from Seat's view is shared between the three BookingButton.

External Data

For managing external Data, SwiftUI has an ObservableObject Protocol. This requires us to declare a var called objectWillChange which requires a Publisher; commonly, we can use a PassThroughSubject. That is all that would be required to conform to the ObservableObject protocol. Then, when the value changes, we need to send a message using the send method on the Publisher. The PassThroughSubject takes two parameters, an Output and a Failure:

Note   PassThroughSubject and some other functions are part of the Combine library and require that we import Combine before we can use them in our code.

```
class BookingStore: ObservableObject {
    var objectWillChange = PassthroughSubject<Void, Never>()

    var bookingName: String = "" {
        didSet { updateUI() }
    }

    var seats: Int = 1 {
        didSet { updateUI() }
    }

    func updateUI() {
        objectWillChange.send()
    }
}
```

In this preceding example, PassthoughSubject is the publisher that will publish events when the bookingName or seats value is changed. We saw in the earlier section the two principles, about the source of truth and that a view creates a dependency for data that it owns. So, with a publisher, we can create a source of truth, and now, we need to create a dependency. This is quite simple, and all we need to do is to simply declare the model as an ObservedObject variable and instantiate it:

```
struct AnotherView: View {
    @ObservedObject var model = BookingStore()

    var body: some View {
        VStack {
            TextField("Your Name", $model.bookingName)
            Stepper("Seats : \(model.seats)",
                    value: $model.seats,
                    in: 1...5)
        }
    }
}
```

This will now allow us to enter the name that is connected to the model's property bookingName and seats with the stepper, with which we can select the number of seats to book. We have set the range from 1 to 5, so we cannot select less than 1 and more than 5 seats. Now, the view with the property wrapper will have an explicit dependency on this and will automatically subscribe to changes of the ObservableObject. It is all automatically managed for us without having to write any code to sync data between the mode and the view.

An important thing to note is that Views are value types (*structs*), and any time we use a reference type (*class*), we should use the ObservedObject, and this way, the view will know of the dependency and update the view based on the data changes.

All we need to do is describe the dependencies to SwiftUI, and the framework does the rest.

State Vs. Bindable

There are a few subtle differences between @State and @ObservableObject. These are important to know as both serve a different purpose. Firstly, @State is local to the view. The value or the Data is held locally in the View. It is managed by the framework, and it is a value type since it is stored locally.

The @ObservableObject on the other hand is External to the view, and it is not stored in the view. It is a reference type as it is not stored locally and simply has a reference to the value. This is not managed automatically by the framework and is the responsibility of the developer to manage it. This works best with external data like a database or a model that is managed by code.

Binding

We know that data immutability is a good practice and read-only access is preferred. It helps cut down a lot of errors and helps provide a faster and efficient experience. A lot of organizations are working toward using immutable interfaces to leverage these benefits. SwiftUI offers immutability for data by default, and for mutable data objects, we can use the @Binding property wrapper.

@Binding is a first-class reference to data; it allows the components to read and write a value without owning it. We can get a binding to a multitude of data, including State, ObservedObject, and even another Binding. To ensure that the binding can read and mutate the value, we need to prefix the variable with the $ sign. That is all, and we have Bindings that works with data. This also helps create separation of concern while eliminating sync issues.

What to Use When

State is not mentioned in separation of concerns or in building reusable components as we saw earlier in the example because States are enclosed inside a view and its children. It might not be the correct option if the value of data comes from somewhere outside of the view. It is a good start to prototype and create a local state and then extract it out and use a binding. Generally, the data models will definitely live outside of the view and be external to the view. This dependency on State can be considered and moved to a Binding or an ObservableObject and managed. This is powerful, but also be mindful of the fact as to who owns the data. As an example, if the button requires to store the background color, it cannot be shared and be stored centrally or externally, that is something that each instance needs to store locally.

Creating Dependencies Indirectly

The model can be moved into the EnvironmentObject, and from there, the dependencies can still be made to views and their subviews which will ensure that the view is updated as soon as the model is changed which is stored in the EnvironmentObject.

Adding a value into the EnvironmentObject is as easy as simply as using the modifier environmentObject and passing it the value:

```
static var previews: some View {
    var store = BookingStore()
    return AnotherObject.environmentObject(store)
}
```

And in the AnotherView instead of using the @ObservedObject, we can replace that with @EnvironmentObject. It does not require to be initialized; it is optional; if it exists in the environment, it is provided to us, and if it doesn't, then the app will crash.

We can use ObservedObject and use it alone for managing the data dependency on the entire view hierarchy. However, the only problem is that the dependency needs to be passed down the hierarchy to the views that require the dependency on the ObservedObject. This is where EnvironmentObject comes in handy; it can provide an indirect dependency to the children directly without having to pass the dependency down the hierarchy. Look at the following diagram to understand the difference between ObservableObject and EnvironmentObject as can be seen in Figure 4-4.

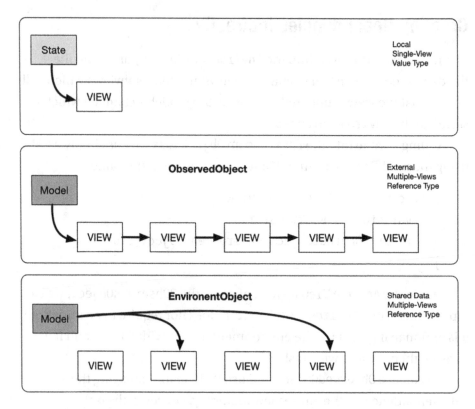

Figure 4-4. *Difference between ObservableObject and EnvironmentObject*

The Environment Object is a *container,* and it can be used across the system in a variety of ways and things like the *Dark Mode, Light Mode, Left-to-Right* and *Right-to-Left* directions, and so on. These are all part of the `Environment,` and the system makes use of them, and so can we in our applications. In some ways, an `EnvironmentObject` is like a Global Variable Container, but Apple does not like calling it that.

Combine

Combine is a unified, declarative API for processing values over time. It is written in and for Swift, hence takes advantage of Swift features like Generics, Type Safe, and Composition.

This chapter would not go into the details of the Combine library but a quick overview of the same. The key concepts of Combine are Publishers and Subscribers.

Publishers are the declarative part of the API; it defines how the values and errors are produced. They are value type and allow for the registration of a Subscriber that receives values over time.

Subscribers are the counterparts to Publishers; they receive values and a completion. They are of reference type because the Subscribers add and mutate state we use as a reference type.

When values are received from a Publisher, they could be in a different format, and we can use Operators to convert those into another format.

We can also use it incrementally piece by piece with UIKit. Combine can also help make the code readable and manageable. It can convert several inputs into a single value that can then be usable. With SwiftUI, we only need to define the dependencies, SwiftUI owns the Subscriber, and we just need a Publisher. To use it, we simply need to conform to the Bindable protocol.

We can simply add a Publisher to any property by simply adding the annotation @Published. This property wrapper adds functionality where it automatically synthesizes the objectWillChange publisher and calls it whenever the value changes.

Summary

In this chapter, we had a look at what is Data and the two principles on which SwiftUI is based with regard to Data, the first being that every time data is referenced by a view, a dependency is created and the other that data is the source of truth that is responsible for the view to be updated. In SwiftUI, the `@State` is this source of truth for data that is local to the view and `@Binding` for a reference to the data from the parent view. `@ObservableObject` can be used for data from a model, and `@Environment` can be used for reference to data that is available in the ancestry of the views. These are all powered by `Property Wrappers` and `Combine`. These can be generally used with Swift too. In the next chapter, we shall look at how we can use SwiftUI for Presentation and Layout.

CHAPTER 5

Layout and Presentation

In the last chapter, we had a look at how Data works in SwiftUI and the principles behind it all. Now that we have a better idea on some of the interesting parts that make SwiftUI work, let's focus our attention now to the visual, interesting part of SwiftUI that allows us to layout our UI and presentation.

Elements and Modifiers

We had a quick and brief introduction to SwiftUI (in earlier chapters) and saw that SwiftUI is a combination of UI elements and modifiers that manipulate the elements as required. We shall use these modifiers to layout our elements.

SwiftUI does not use AutoLayout in the traditional sense. It is used for laying out elements behind the scenes, but not exposed to the developers. SwiftUI uses a flexible box layout system that is commonly used with Java and web development.

We no longer have to set up constraints and wire up attributes to set up the application layout. Instead with the modifiers, we can do a lot more than we could before.

© Jayant Varma 2019
J. Varma, *SwiftUI for Absolute Beginners*, https://doi.org/10.1007/978-1-4842-5516-2_5

Modifiable Attributes

In a brief introduction to the elements, we saw how each of the *UIElements* are viewed and that they have modifiers that change or set some values of the element. A simple example that we can see is that of Text; we can simply display test by using the keyword Text as

```
Text("Hello World")
```

We can further modify that by changing the background color simply by using the modifier `.background` as

```
Text("Hello World")
.background(Color.red)
```

This sets a red background to the text *Hello World*, clipped to the size of the Text. We can add a little padding to the text, with

```
Text("Hello World")
.padding()
.background(Color.red)
```

This adds a little padding around the Text. Note that the text label on the screen is a nice rectangle with a red background. We can also modify this further by making it rounded using the `.cornerRadius` modifier:

```
Text("Hello World")
.padding()
.background(Color.red)
.cornerRadius(10.0)
```

Modifiers can be chained, and they act incrementally on the already present modified attributes. So, we can add these together to form a Rainbow:

```
struct RainbowText: View {
    private let radius: CGFloat = 25.0
```

```
var body: some View {
      Text("Rainbow")
      .padding()
      .background(Color.red)
      .cornerRadius(radius)
      .padding()
      .background(Color.orange)
      .cornerRadius(radius)
      .padding()
      .background(Color.yellow)
      .cornerRadius(radius)
      .padding()
      .background(Color.green)
      .cornerRadius(radius)
      .padding()
      .background(Color.blue)
      .cornerRadius(radius)
      .padding()
      .background(Color.purple)
      .cornerRadius(radius)
   }
}
```

And just like that, we get a set of rainbow-colored concentric rectangles as seen in Figure 5-1. The way to look at this is that each element is a view; even a modifier sends back a view. This way, the chaining can work on the view applying the attributes as modified via the modifiers.

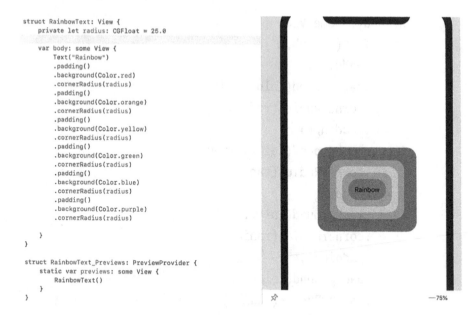

```
struct RainbowText: View {
    private let radius: CGFloat = 25.0

    var body: some View {
        Text("Rainbow")
        .padding()
        .background(Color.red)
        .cornerRadius(radius)
        .padding()
        .background(Color.orange)
        .cornerRadius(radius)
        .padding()
        .background(Color.yellow)
        .cornerRadius(radius)
        .padding()
        .background(Color.green)
        .cornerRadius(radius)
        .padding()
        .background(Color.blue)
        .cornerRadius(radius)
        .padding()
        .background(Color.purple)
        .cornerRadius(radius)

    }
}

struct RainbowText_Previews: PreviewProvider {
    static var previews: some View {
        RainbowText()
    }
}
```

Figure 5-1. *Rainbow-colored text*

Similarly, we can also use circles to create a concentric colored circle as seen in Figure 5-2. It is as simple as the following code snippet:

```
struct ColoredCircles: View {
    var body: some View {
        ZStack {
            Circle().fill(Color.green)
            Circle().fill(Color.yellow).scaleEffect(0.8)
            Circle().fill(Color.orange).scaleEffect(0.6)
            Circle().fill(Color.red).scaleEffect(0.4)
        }
    }
}
```

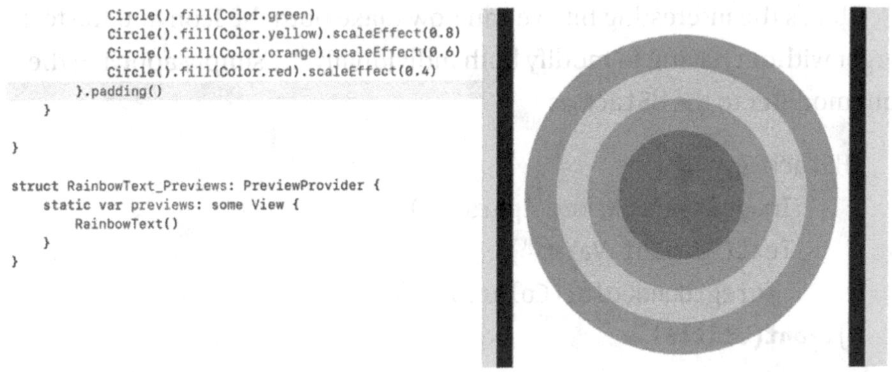

```
            Circle().fill(Color.green)
            Circle().fill(Color.yellow).scaleEffect(0.8)
            Circle().fill(Color.orange).scaleEffect(0.6)
            Circle().fill(Color.red).scaleEffect(0.4)
        }.padding()
    }
}

struct RainbowText_Previews: PreviewProvider {
    static var previews: some View {
        RainbowText()
    }
}
```

Figure 5-2. *Concenteric circles*

Stacking Views

We also saw earlier that we could use one of the two stack options HStack or VStack to stack elements together *horizontally* or *vertically*. This is most commonly used for things like the TabView, Segments, and TableCells. We can start with creating a user account control, which has an icon of a person and the name of the logged in user:

```
struct UserNameControl: View {
    HStack {
        Image(systemName: "person")
        Text("Jayant Varma")
    }
}
```

We can further change this by adding a color to the username using a foregroundColor modifier:

```
HStack {
    Image(systemName: "person")
    Text("Jayant Varma")
    .foregroundColor(Color.blue)
}
```

71

Here's the interesting bit, we can now make both the Icon and the text larger without having to modify both individually, by simply applying the font modifier to the HStack as

```
HStack {
    Image(systemName: "person")
    Text("Jayant Varma")
    .foregroundColor(Color.blue)
}.font(.title)
```

This now creates the simplest Control that displays the name of the user and an image preceding it as seen in Figure 5-3. We do not have to align, set the distances, and so on. It is all done for us automagically by SwiftUI. Note that the last line applies a font of type title to the entire HStack, so it gets applied to both the icon and the text.

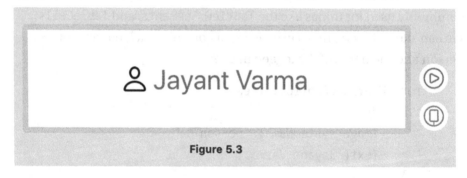

Figure 5.3

Figure 5-3. *The username and the icon as a single control*

Creating Image Assets

Say we wanted to make a large-sized Image, this would be quite a lot of effort with other languages including Swift in drawing it ourselves. With SwiftUI, we can do so easily as per the following code in Figure 5-4:

```swift
struct IconMaker: View {

    var body: some View {
        Image(systemName: "cloud.sun.bolt.fill")
        .resizable()
        .frame(width: 250, height: 250)
          .padding()
          .foregroundColor(Color.white)
          .background(LinearGradient(
            gradient: Gradient(colors:
                [Color.yellow, Color.orange]),
            startPoint: .top,
            endPoint: .bottom))
        .cornerRadius(30)
        .shadow(radius: 10)
    }

}
```

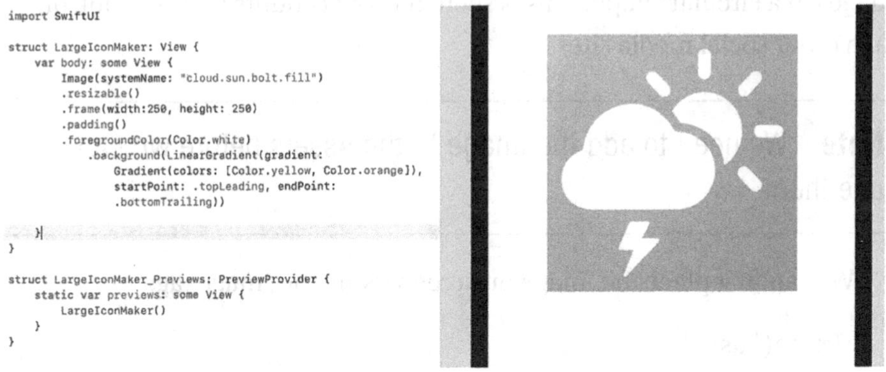

Figure 5-4. *The large Icon created via code*

This is a good example of simply adding modifiers to the element to reach an interesting outcome.

The first thing that we did is make the image *resizable*; the moment we do that, the image gets a modifier of aspectFill and the size would fill the entire screen. Next, we create a frame that is a square to have the correct aspect ratio and not stretch or squash the icon. Then, we added a padding so that the icon has a little space around it and then set the color to white and the background to a gradient that starts from *topLeft* to *bottomRight* (*Diagonally*) and is a gradient of the colors from yellow to orange. The gradient element takes three parameters, gradient, startPoint, and endPoint. The *start* and the *end* point determine how the gradient grades the color, that is, the direction of the gradient, from top to bottom, from leading to trailing or topLeading to bottomTrailing. The *gradient* takes a Gradient object that has an array of colors in use:

```
Gradient(colors: [Color.yellow, Color.orange])
```

Clipping Images

One more very common UI element that we see in most applications are images in a circular shape. This is seen in user accounts on Facebook or such other social media sites.

Note   We need to add the image to the Assets before we can use them.

We can first place the image on screen using the Image tag:

```
Image("user")
```

Next, we can clip the image into a circular shape; however, if the image was large, then we need to resize it to what we need on the screen, and we can achieve that using resizable and a frame modifier as we did earlier. Then, we can clip it using a clipShape using a Circle() shape as can be seen in Figure 5-5:

```
Image("user")
.resizable()
.frame(width: 250, height: 250)
.clipShape(Circle())
```

We can create a border for this by adding an overlay using the Overlay modifier and adding a Circle on top this image and then stroke it with a color:

```
Image("user")
.resizable()
.aspectRatio(contentMode: .fill)
.frame(width: 250, height: 250)
.clipShape(Circle())
.overlay(
  Circle().stroke(Color.black, lineWidth: 2)
)
.shadow(10)
```

```
import SwiftUI

struct CustomUser: View {
    var body: some View {
        Image("user")
        .resizable()
        .aspectRatio(contentMode: .fill)
        .frame(width: 250, height: 250)
        .clipShape(Circle())
        .overlay(
        Circle().stroke(Color.black, lineWidth: 2)
        )
            .shadow(radius: 10)
    }
}

struct CustomUser_Previews: PreviewProvider {
    static var previews: some View {
        CustomUser()
    }
}
```

Figure 5-5. *A User profile clipped in a circle as used in many apps*

Composition

The basis on which SwiftUI was created was to make it more of a composition-based language, and it is not only with the UI but also the other bits like operators, modifiers, combine operators, and so on.

We can now add the user details with the image to form an interface that we are after:

```
VStack {
    Text("Jayant Varma")
        .font(.largeTitle)
    Text("http://www.oz-apps.com")
}
```

We can place that in a VStack and then add the Image in another VStack to add it above the user details as seen in Figure 5-6:

```
VStack {
    Image("user")
    .resizable()
    .frame(width: 250, height: 250)
    .clipShape(Circle())
    .overlay(
      Circle().stroke(Color.blue, lineWidth: 2)
    )
    .shadow(10)
}
VStack {
    Text("Jayant Varma")
        .font(.largeTitle)
    Text("http://www.oz-apps.com")
}
```

```
VStack {
    Image("user")
        .resizable()
        .aspectRatio(contentMode: .fill)
        .frame(width: 250, height: 250)
        .clipShape(Circle())
        .overlay(
            Circle().stroke(Color.black,
                lineWidth: 2)
        )
        .shadow(radius: 10)
    VStack {
        Text("Jayant Varma")
            .font(.largeTitle)
        Text("http://www.oz-apps.com")
    }
}
}
}

struct CustomUser_Previews: PreviewProvider {
    static var previews: some View {
```

Jayant Varma
http://www.oz-apps.com

Figure 5-6.   *User Account custom view*

From within Xcode, we can also extract this entire section as a custom
view. This can then be reused as we did in the previous chapter when
we were creating reusable buttons. We can do so by selecting the section
and then either selecting the menu options from the Editor menu, Extract
to Method or Extract to Variable as seen in Figure 5-7 or by clicking the
element with the Command button pressed as seen in Figure 5-8 and
selecting the *Extract Subview* option.

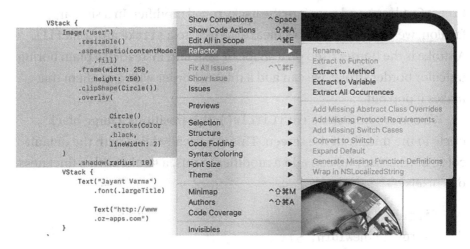

Figure 5-7.   *Menu-based option from the Editor menu*

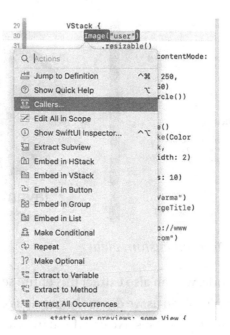

Figure 5-8. *Context menu with the Command button pressed*

Gradients

We saw that we can use gradient backgrounds by simply using a
LinearGradient and pass it to the background modifier. In a similar
fashion, we can also assign a LinearGradient to a stroke and/or a fill.
A stroke is the border used on a shape or text, and instead of a plain boring
unicolor border stroke, we can add a thicker border with a gradient that
makes it pop out.

We can create a circle with Circle(); this positions a large black
circle in the middle of the screen. This is basically filled with the default
color, black. Next, we can add a modifier to this, a stroke with a thickness
of 5 pixels:

```
Circle()
.stroke(linewidth: 5)
```

We can see that now the circle has a border with a thickness of 5 pixels but not filled. If we change this to a larger number like 25, we get a thick solid border that can benefit from a gradient color on it:

```
Circle()
.stroke(
    LinearGradient(gradient: Gradient(colors:[.red, .blue]),
        startPoint: .top,
        endPoint: .bottom),
        linewidth: 25)
```

This will create a gradient circle for us of 25 pixel thickness as can be seen in Figure 5-9.

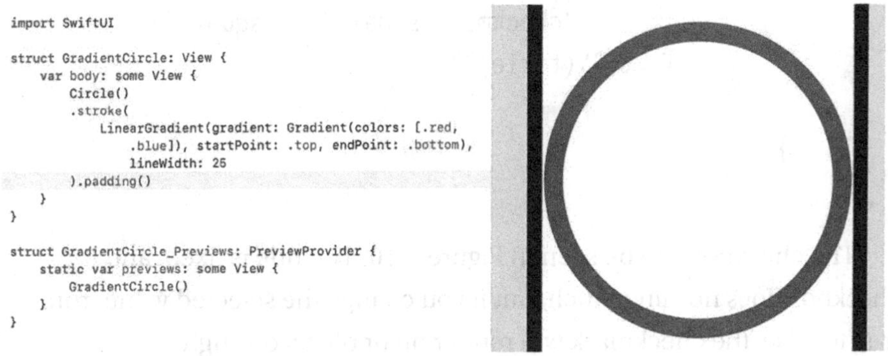

```
import SwiftUI

struct GradientCircle: View {
    var body: some View {
        Circle()
        .stroke(
            LinearGradient(gradient: Gradient(colors: [.red,
                .blue]), startPoint: .top, endPoint: .bottom),
                lineWidth: 25
        ).padding()
    }
}

struct GradientCircle_Previews: PreviewProvider {
    static var previews: some View {
        GradientCircle()
    }
}
```

Figure 5-9. *A circle with a gradient stroke*

Creating a Check Box

While we are looking at custom, composable UI, we shall try to make a check box that displays a checkmark when selected and just the square when not. This can be used in a more common example like *ToDo lists*. So, let's get started; first, we create a new View and add a @State to hold the value of the selection:

```
struct CheckBox: some View {
    @State private var selected: Bool = false
    var title: String = "untitled"

    var body: some View {
        HStack {
            Image(systemName: selected ?
                    "checkmark.square" : "square")
            Text("\(title)")
        }
    }
}
```

The checkbox can be seen in Figure 5-10. The title is fixed, and the checkbox does nothing much, but if you change the selected value from true to false, the checkmark will render on or off accordingly.

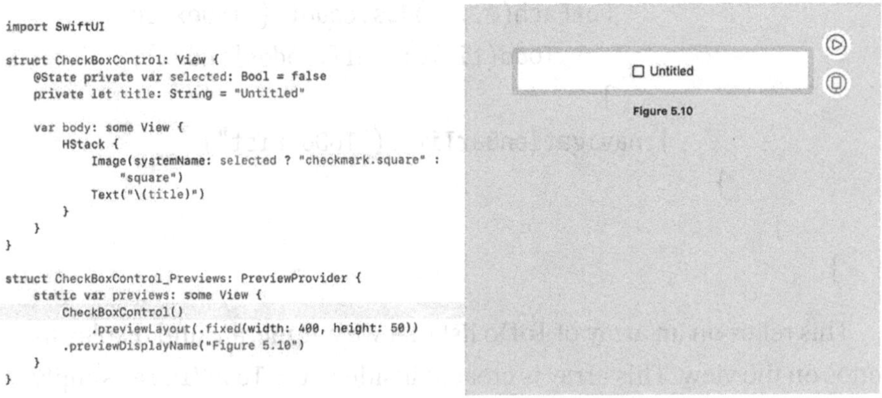

```
import SwiftUI

struct CheckBoxControl: View {
    @State private var selected: Bool = false
    private let title: String = "Untitled"

    var body: some View {
        HStack {
            Image(systemName: selected ? "checkmark.square" :
                "square")
            Text("\(title)")
        }
    }
}

struct CheckBoxControl_Previews: PreviewProvider {
    static var previews: some View {
        CheckBoxControl()
            .previewLayout(.fixed(width: 400, height: 50))
        .previewDisplayName("Figure 5.10")
    }
}
```

☐ Untitled

Figure 5.10

Figure 5-10.   *Create a checkbox – version 1*

We can also add some interaction to this by simply adding a tapGesture handler to it, which will change the selection and thereby toggle the checkmark or the square:

```
var body: some View {
    HStack {
        Image(systemName: selected ?
                "checkmark.square" : "square")
        Text("\(title)")
    }.onTapGesture {
        self.selected.toggle()
    }
}
```

Now, we can use this in an actual todo type application where we can very easily create a todo list:

```
struct ToDoView: some View {
    var body: some View {
        NavigationView {
            List {
```

```
            ForEach(0..<todos.count){ index in
                Todo(title: self.todos[index])
            }
        }.navigationBarTitle("ToDo List")
    }
  }
}
```

This relies on an array of ToDo list that we enumerate and display as Todos on the view. This array is created inside of the ToDoView as simply as the following code. In a runtime, we might pass it an array of a structure ToDo or a viewModel:

```
let todos = [
    "Check email",
    "Feed the dogs",
    "Write another chapter",
    "Watch another episode",
    "Add mor eimages to the chapters",
    "Walk for 30 minutes"
]
```

Now, if we either run or preview this ToDoView, we get the list of Todos listed with a blank square, and if we tap on the item, it checks the checkbox, and on tapping it again, it removes the checkmark as can be seen in Figure 5-11.

```
import SwiftUI

let todos = [
    "Check email",
    "Feed the dogs",
    "Write another chapter",
    "Watch another episode",
    "Add more images to the chapters",
    "Walk for 30 minutes"
]

struct TodoView: View {
    var body: some View {
        NavigationView {
            List {
                ForEach(0..<todos.count) { index in
                    Todo(title: todos[index])
                }
            }
            .navigationBarTitle("ToDo List")
        }
    }
}

struct TodoView_Previews: PreviewProvider {
    static var previews: some View {
        TodoView()
        .previewDevice("iPhone SE")
    }
}
```

Figure 5-11. *The Todo list view running with a couple of items striken off*

We can also draw a strikethrough on the text to indicate that the task is completed. This is simply achieved by adding a modifier to the Text element in the Todo declaration as

```
Text("\(title)")
    .strikethrough(selected, color: .red)
```

This could be further expanded to create a simple todo program; however, we would not pursue that in this chapter/book. It is an exercise left for the reader.

Composing Multiple Items

We have seen bits and pieces for creating UI elements; SwiftUI makes it quite easy, and it can also be extended to TableViews or ListViews, repeating data in a scrollable table-like manner. In many apps, developers create Thumbnails that have an image in the background with a text overlay, and these are generally scrollable left to right.

So, we create this Just Desserts scroller incrementally which will demonstrate how we can use SwiftUI to compose and refactor. We create a new SwiftUI file called Thumbnail. In the body, we can place the following code listed. The images are all saved in the Assets for the purpose of this example:

```
var body: some View {
    VStack {
        Image("cheesecake")
        .resizable()
        .frame(width: 350, height: 250)
        .aspectRatio(contentMode: .fill)
        .cornerRadius(15)
    }
}
```

This creates a card for our images as can be seen in Figure 5-12.

Figure 5-12. *The basic Dessert Card*

We can now place the text on top of this with a Text element:

```
VStack {
    Image("cheesecake")
    ...
    Text("Baked Cheesecake")
```

```
        .font(.title)
        .bold()
        .foregroundColor(.white)
        .padding()
    }
```

We use the white font because it needs to be visible on top of the image. However, since these are placed in a VStack, it displays below the image on a white background and hence is not seen. So, let us first change the VStack to a ZStack; that way, the text will be placed atop the image, but in the center. We can fix that by changing the alignment of the ZStack as

```
ZStack(alignment: .bottomLeading)
```

The Text could still be not clearly visible as the image may have elements of a lighter color that merge with the text as can be seen in Figure 5-13.

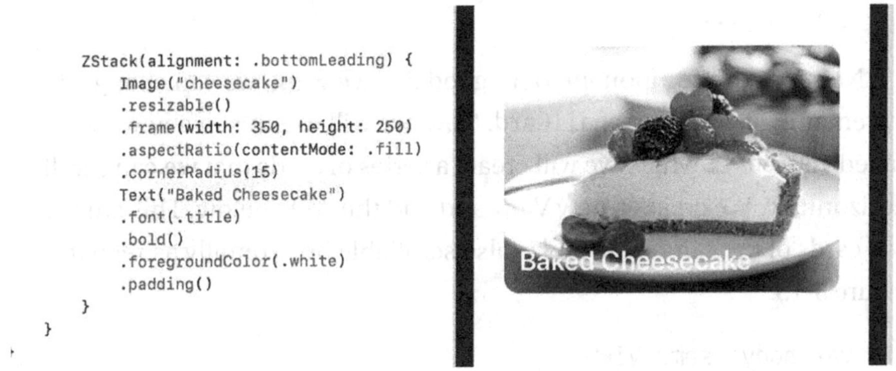

```
ZStack(alignment: .bottomLeading) {
    Image("cheesecake")
    .resizable()
    .frame(width: 350, height: 250)
    .aspectRatio(contentMode: .fill)
    .cornerRadius(15)
    Text("Baked Cheesecake")
    .font(.title)
    .bold()
    .foregroundColor(.white)
    .padding()
    }
}
```

Figure 5-13. *Added a text on top of the basic card*

To fix that issue, we can add a black rectangle below which can provide a dark background to the text just between the Image and the text using the RoundedRectangle element as seen in Figure 5-14.

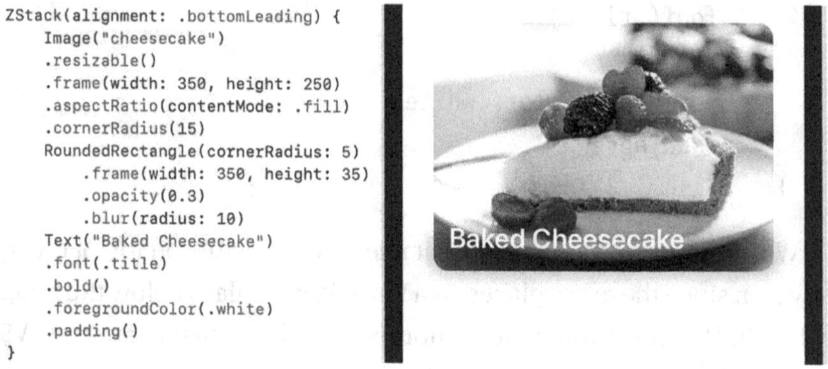

```
ZStack(alignment: .bottomLeading) {
    Image("cheesecake")
    .resizable()
    .frame(width: 350, height: 250)
    .aspectRatio(contentMode: .fill)
    .cornerRadius(15)
    RoundedRectangle(cornerRadius: 5)
        .frame(width: 350, height: 35)
        .opacity(0.3)
        .blur(radius: 10)
    Text("Baked Cheesecake")
    .font(.title)
    .bold()
    .foregroundColor(.white)
    .padding()
}
```

Figure 5-14. *The card looking much better with the text popping*

```
    ...
RoundedRectangle(cornerRadius: 5)
    .frame(width: 350, height: 35)
    .opacity(0.35)
    .blur(radius: 10)
Text("Baked Cheesecake")
    ...
```

Now that the component looks good like we want, we can change it by renaming it as a ThumbnailCard. Now, we will use this in a new view called Thumbnail which we will create a series of cards that we can scroll horizontally. We create a new View and add the code below. This creates five cards of the same type and is also scrollable horizontally as seen in Figure 5-15:

```
var body: some View {
    VStack(alignment: .leading) {
        Text("Just Desserts")
            .font(.largeTitle)
            .padding()
```

```
ScrollView(.horizontal, showsIndicators: false) {
    HStack {
        ForEach(0..<5) { index in
            ThumbnailCard()
        }
    }.padding()
    }
}
}
```

```
struct ThumbnailBasicView: View {
    var body: some View {
        VStack {
            Text("Just Desserts")
            .font(.largeTitle)
            .padding()
            ScrollView(.horizontal,
                showsIndicators: false) {
                HStack {
                    ForEach(0..<5) { index in
                        ThumbnailCard()
                    }
                }.padding()
            }
        }
    }
}
```

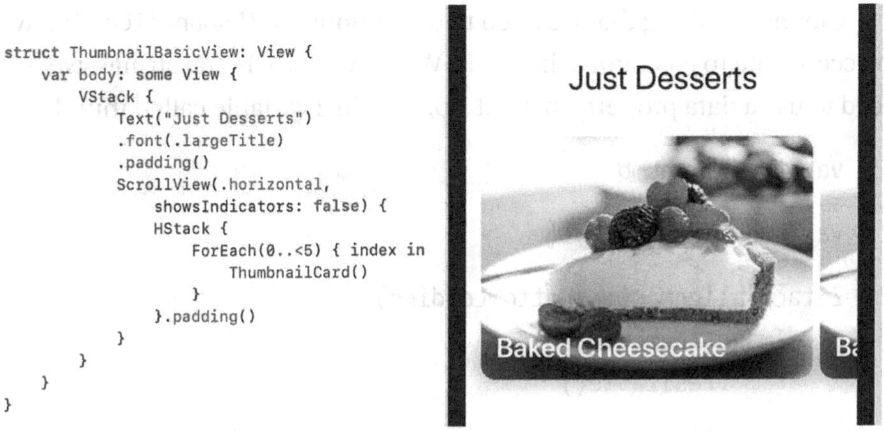

Figure 5-15. *A horizontally scrollable list of Dessert Cards*

This is easier than using a UICollectionView. We still have another issue, that is, the cards themselves. We need a way that we can have different cards. If we were to use this in our project, we would have had a series of images and text from a data model. So, let's create a *dataModel* to hold this information; it's simple and looks like

```
struct Thumb {
    var title: String
    var image: String
}
```

Now, we can create an array of Thumbs which will provide the data to our view:

```
let thumbnailData = [
    Thumb(title:"Baked Cheesecake", image:"cheesecake"),
    Thumb(title:"Caramel Tart", image:"caramel"),
    Thumb(title:"Fudge Ice cream", image:"fudgeicecream"),
    Thumb(title:"Passionberry Cake", image:"passionberry"),
    Thumb(title:"Tiramisu", image:"tiramisu")
]
```

And the last thing that we need to do is adopt the ThumbnailCard view to accept data to customize the cards. Where we have literal strings, we need to use a data property instead. So, we add a variable called thumb:

```
var thumb: Thumb

var body: some View {

ZStack(alignment: .bottomLeading) {
    Image(thumb.image)
        .resizable()
        ...
    Text("\(thumb.title)")
        ...
}
```

And we need to pass the data to this view when we call it in the ScrollView as can be seen in Figure 5-16:

```
ScrollView(.horizontal, showsIndicators: false) {
    HStack {
        ForEach(0..<thumbnailData.count) { index in
            ThumbnailCard(thumb: thumbnailData[index])
        }
```

```
    }.padding()
}
```

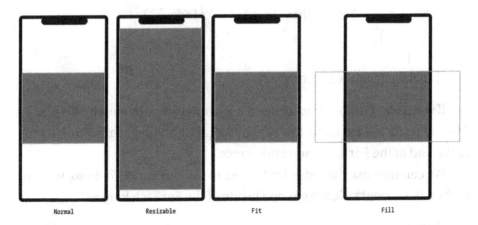

Figure 5-16. *Just Desserts with the images laid out*

Normal	Resizable	Fit	Fill

Figure 5-17. *Image and its modifiers*

Here's a quick reckoner of how the images look when used with
different modifiers and when we use them for sizing the images as seen in
Figure 5-17.

Layouts

One last thing before we finish the chapter is to know about
GeometryReader. This is used to provide geometry for the layouts of
elements. Apple defines this as *A container view that defines it content as
a function of its own size and coordinate space. Returns a flexible preferred
size to its parent layout.*

We can quickly see the way it helps us to use a GeometryReader. We
can create a ScrollView and inside add a number of Text elements that can
be scrolled horizontally:

```
ScrollView {
    HStack {
        ForEach(0..<15){ index in
            Text("This is item: \(index)")
        }
    }
}.background(Color.orange)
```

If we set on *LivePreview*, we see a horizontally scrollable list of 'This is
item n' texts. We can make this slightly larger by adding a frame modifier
at the end of the ForEach loop curly brace.

We can now use the GeometryReader to use the same. To do so, we can
embed the GeometryReader Scope inside of the ForEach loop as

```
ScrollView {
    HStack {
        ForEach(0..<15){ index in
            GeometryReader { g in
                Text("This is item: \(index)")
                    .rotationEffect(.degrees(
                        Double(g.frame(in: .global).minX)
                    ))
```

```
        }
    }.frame(width: 300, height: 300)
  }
}.background(Color.orange)
```

Now when we scroll, the label rotates or rather tumbles circularly as it scrolls. This is because the GeometryReader provides the frame reference at each stage of the scrolling position.

In the preceding code, we are using the geometry object to get the frame in reference to the global and get the minX from that.

Summary

In this chapter, we have seen many ways to compose and create custom views and lay them in relation to each other as a vertically scrolling list and as horizontally scrolling cells, and use icons and text. SwiftUI is based on the premise that views can be composed and added together to form complex layouts. We can use various methods to store and pass data locally within the view, or between views. In the next chapter, we shall look at Drawing and Animation using SwiftUI.

CHAPTER 6

Drawing and Animation

We have looked at some of the elements and functionality of SwiftUI. While we have seen how to create lovely interfaces with composition, it could add a bit of pop if these could be alive. Animation brings the elements to life and makes them more interesting. In this chapter, we shall see some interesting ways to animate and make the elements interesting.

Timers

The traditional way of animation is to use a timer. The theory behind this is that the timer fires every number of seconds that we want, and when this timer fires, we can run the code to update or alter the properties of the elements either the position, the scale, the opacity, or others.

The first thing to start a timer-based animation is to have a timer. In SwiftUI, timers can be a publisher as they publish a steady stream of values as per the duration set on the timer:

```
let timer = Timer.publish(every: 1, on: .current, in: .common).
autoconnect()
```

© Jayant Varma 2019
J. Varma, *SwiftUI for Absolute Beginners*, https://doi.org/10.1007/978-1-4842-5516-2_6

Next, we can receive this value in any element by using the onReceive method. Our code to display a timer would look like

```
struct TimerView: View {
    @State private var counter = 0
    let timer = Timer.publish(every: 1, on: current, in:
    .common).autoconnect()

    var body: some View {
        Text("Counter Ticks : \(counter)")
            .onReceive(timer) { _ in
                self.counter += 1
            }
    }
}
```

In the preview, we cannot see it running; however when we click on the Live Preview, button that looks like a play button as seen in Figure 6-1, we can see it running and previewing right in XCode.

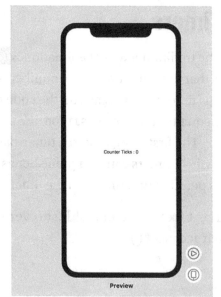

Figure 6-1. *Timer Animation text*

Making It Better

We can make better use of timer now that we know that we can get the
timer event every 1 second. We can take the concentric-colored circles that
we created in our last chapter, and we can use that and animate it:

```
struct AnimatedView: View {
    @State private var flipFlop = false

    let timer = Timer.publish(every: 1, on: .current,
                    in: .common).autoconnect()

    var body: some View {
        ZStack {
            Circle().fill(Color.green)
            Circle().fill(Color.yellow)
                .scaleEffect(0.8)
            Circle().fill(Color.orange)
                .scaleEffect(0.6)
            Circle().fill(Color.red)
                .scaleEffect(0.4)
        }
        .scaleEffect(flipFlop ? 0.2 : 0.8)
        .opacity(flipFlop ? 0.1 : 1.0)
        .animation(Animation.spring()
                .repeatForever(autoreverses: true))
        .onReceive(timer) { _ in
            self.flipFlip.toggle()
        }
    }
}
```

And now, if we run the app or the *LivePreview*, we can see the circles shrink and fade and then zoom out and back on indefinitely. We set up the animation and set it to run forever, and when the animation is completed, we asked it to reverse the animation. This can be seen in Figure 6-2.

```
var body: some View {
    ZStack {
        Circle()
            .fill(Color.green)
        Circle()
            .fill(Color.yellow)
            .scaleEffect(0.8)
        Circle()
            .fill(Color.orange)
            .scaleEffect(0.6)
        Circle()
            .fill(Color.red)
            .scaleEffect(0.4)
    }
    .scaleEffect(flipFlop ? 0.2: 0.8)
    .opacity(flipFlop ? 0.1 : 1.0)
    .animation(Animation.spring()
        .repeatForever(autoreverses: true))
    .onReceive(timer) {_ in
        self.flipFlop.toggle()
        }
    }
}

struct TimerView_Previews: PreviewProvider {
    static var previews: some View {
        TimerView()
    }
}
```

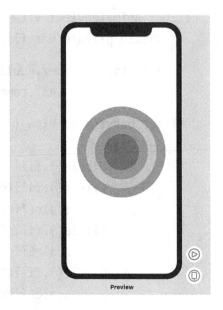

Figure 6-2. *Concentric circles that animate their scale and opacity*

Shapes

In the examples we have used some shapes like a Circle and a Rectangle. SwiftUI offers some more shapes and modifier that allow us to create more from those. Let us look at some of the shapes that we can create.

Rectangle

The simplest and the most common shape that we can create is a Rectangle. And the easiest way to create a rectangle is using the Rectangle element:

```
Rectangle()
```

This takes no parameters and creates a filled rectangle on the screen. All of the standard modifiers are applicable to these like background, foregroundColor, scale, frame, and so on.

RoundedRectangle

A variation on the Rectangle is the RoundedRectangle. This is similar to a rectangle, but the corners are not as sharp as in a rectangle but rounded. This rounding radius can be specified when creating the element. A RoundedRectangle can be created with either a cornerRadius or a cornerSize where we can change the radius for the width and the height:

```
RoundedRectangle(cornerRadius: 35)
RoundedRectangle(cornerSize: CGSize(width: 60, height: 30))
```

Circle

The next shape that we can look at is the Circle; its function is quite simple and creates a circle on the screen:

```
Circle()
```

There are some variations of Circles that we will look at next.

Ellipse

The first variation of a Circle is the Ellipse; this is a stretched circle in the rectangular frame. The Ellipse is an oval that can look pointy in comparison to a circle. There are no parameters passed when creating an Ellipse, and the element name is Ellipse:

```
Ellipse()
```

Capsule

Another variation of the Circle is a Capsule. This is different from an Ellipse by the fact that it does not look like a stretched Circle, but a Circle that has a solid Rectangle in the middle. It looks like a capsule or a RoundedRect with high cornerRadius.

Custom Corners for RoundedRectangle

While we can create rectangles with custom corners, we can also create rectangles with custom corners rounded. While there is no out-of-the-box shape that does this, we can still create something by using Paths, something that we will look into further in this chapter. Since this would use UIBezierCurve to get a path, we can create a Path Object from this bezier path's cgPath property:

```
Path(
    UIBezierPath(
        roundedRect:
            CGRect(
                origin: .zero,
                size: CGSize(width: 100, height: 50)),
        byRoundingCorners: [.topRight, .bottomLeft],
        cornerRadii: CGSize(width: 15, height: 15)
    ).cgPath
)
.fill(Color.red)
```

This preceding code will create a Red rectangle with the topRight and the bottomLeft corners rounded. This can be used to selectively round only the corners that we want to round. The output of this can be seen in Figure 6-3. We can also specify the *corner radius,* but we have to pass it as a CGSize instead. This determines how much do we want to curve the corners.

Figure 6-3. *The custom rounded rectangle using Bezier Paths*

Shape Modifiers

The second part of drawing shapes is modifying them, some of them that help us create more complex shapes from these. These are generally chained together to create complex outcomes. We have already used some of these earlier and seen them in action too. However, let us go through them in detail.

Frame

The first and most important modifier is frame; this allows us to specify a frame or a boundingRect that specifies the size in which the shape is drawn. This is to create fixed size shapes like we did in the previous chapters to draw icons and the like.

Clipped

This is something that can be a lifesaver; content can overflow from the frame bounds when we are dealing with Paths and shapes; however, if we want to constraint the content and clip them, we can use the .clipped() modifier. This will ensure that the contents are the size of the container frame.

Trim

The other modifier is trim; this is used to cut the shape at the points where we can pass to the modifier. It requires two parameters, namely, from and to. These allow us to cut the shape accordingly. In terms of a circle, these are generally 4 points between 0 and 1, namely, between 0.0 to 0.5, 0.25 to 0.75, and 0.5 to 1.0; the other values don't work well with circles as can be seen in Figure 6-4 and with rectangles in Figure 6-5.

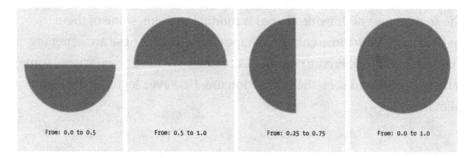

Figure 6-4. The trim values for circles

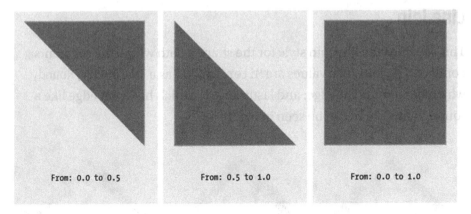

Figure 6-5. *The trim values for Rectangles*

Stroke

Another modifier that we can use with shapes is stroke; this is quite interesting because the moment we apply a stroke, the shape loses the fill and just had the border. This is pretty useful to create outlines for shapes. The stroke modifier takes a linewidth or could take a `lineStyle`; this is useful in creating dashed or dotted lines:

```
Rectangle()
.stroke(linewidth: 10)
```

We can now try to draw dotted lines instead of the solid outline; it is as easy as creating a `StrokeStyle`. A `StrokeStyle` includes the `linewidth` but also takes some additional parameters like the `lineCap` as can be seen in Figure 6-6.

LineCap

This specifies the shape of the endpoints of an open path when stroked. These values can include `Butt`, which has square sharp edges but no padding; `Round,` which has rounded edges and padding; and lastly `Square,` which had sharp edges and padding as can be seen in Figure 6-6.

LineJoin

This specifies the line join style for the shape's path where the segments connect. The join style values are Miter, which has a sharp edge; Round, which has a rounded edge; and lastly Bevel, which has a flat edge like a round joint style as can be seen in Figure 6-6.

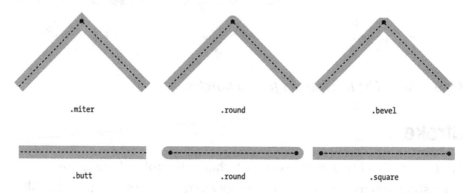

Figure 6-6. *Line Cap and LineJoin types*

Dash

This is the pattern that we can set for the line style. This is an array of numbers that specify the lengths of the painted and unpainted segments. The array has to have even values as the first value is the length of the line and the second value is the length of the gap. So, a perfectly dashed line would have a value of say 5, 5 equal width and equal gap. If we wanted a dashed dotted line, we could use values like 4,4,10,4,4,2,2,2. It's easy to play by changing the values in the code.

DashPhase

This is like an offset and applied to move or offset the start of the pattern when the line starts. This is also used to create the marching ants pattern that we see with some applications.

Using It All

We can use all of the preceding information to create the marching ants pattern as we discussed:

```
Rectangle()
.stroke(style: StrokeStyle(
    lineWidth: 2,
    lineCap: .round,
    lineJoin: .round
    dash: [0, 5],
    dashPhase: 0
    )
)
.frame(width: 200, height: 200)
```

This creates a `Rectangle` with a dotted line; we can animate this if we want and use the `Timer` as we did at the start of this chapter. We can simply pass a value to the `dashPhase` that will change the offset and provide the impression that it is moving.

Animation

Like most of the other features in SwiftUI, animation is also now made easier. In fact, it is now another modifier that we can chain to any Element and pass the type of animation that we want. We have used it in the preceding code, but let us look at it again:

```
Text("Hello World!")
.animation()
```

Nothing happens; that is correct because animation needs some change that should be animated. It also needs to have two states for those changes, a starting state and an end state. At both these states, the property

that we want to animate should change; so say we wanted this to zoom
in and out, we need to play with the scaleEffect property and pass it a
zoomed out and a zoomed in value. We need to have a @State to manage
this value:

```
@State private var jiggle = false

Text("Hello World!")
    .scaleEffect(jiggle ? 1.0 : 0.3)
    .animation(.spring())
```

And even now we have nothing, the reason being very simple, the scale
renders the text the first time and there's nothing more to do. If we could
change the scale by affecting the value of the jiggle variable, we could get it
to change. We can do that with the .onAppear method:

```
Text("Hello World!")
    .scaleEffect(jiggle ? 1.0 : 0.3)
    .animation(.spring())
    .onAppear() { self.jiggle.toggle() }
```

Now we see some movement, but it is still not animating, and that is
because it does it once and stops; if we want it to keep on animating, we
can assign the .repeatForever or a .repeatCount with the number of
times we want to repeat this animation:

```
Text("Hello World!")
    .scaleEffect(jiggle ? 1.0 : 0.3)
    .animation(
        Animation.spring()
            .repeatForever()
    )
    .onAppear() { self.jiggle.toggle() }
```

We can see that it keeps on animating; however, it seems like a blink; it zooms in and disappears to zoom in again. We can now leverage this better by adding an autoreverses parameter and set it to true:

```
.repeatForever(autoreverses: true)
```

And now, we have a smoother animation that zooms in and out and also hope that we have learned about how we can repeat animations. We can also chain effects like adding a 3D rotation, or opacity to have fades like we did at the start of this chapter.

Marching Ants

One of the most common animations that is seen on software is the marching ants, the little animated dotted lines that keep moving around a selection. This is one of the easiest things to create. The first thing is a shape; then, we can stroke it using a dashed line as we saw just earlier and then use the dashPhase property to animate this:

```
Rectangle()
.stroke(Color.red, style: StrokeStyle(
    lineWidth: 2, lineCap: .butt, lineJoin: .round,
    dash: [10, 10], dashPhase: 0))
.frame(width: 300, height: 300)
```

This will not animate as we need to provide it two values, a start and an end value to animate between. So, we can create a @State variable that allows us to animate this:

```
@State private var startAnimating = false
```

And then add the following code in the Rectangle declaration:

```
.animation(Animation.linear(duration: 1.0)
            .repeatsForever(autoreverses: false).speed(4)
.onAppear(){ self.startAnimating.toggle() }
```

We still don't have a change in value, which we can do with changing the dashPhase as

```
dashPhase: startAnimating ? 0: 40
```

Implicit Animation

Another way to animate through a range of values is to use the WithAnimation closure and a @State variable:

```
// First the variable to hold the start value
@State private var changeValue = 0.0

// Now we can assign this to some object (not seen here)

// Lastly we set up the onAppear animation block
.onAppear() {
    WithAnimation {
        self.changeValue = 1.0
    }
}
```

This will pass the values from 0.0 to 1.0 to the changes as can be seen in the following code:

```
@State private var changeValue: CGFloat = 0.0

Text("Hello World!")
    .scaleEffect(changeValue)
    .onAppear() {
        WithAnimation {
            self.changeValue = 1.8
        }
    }
```

And we can see that the text label animates zooming in, much easier and simpler.

Animation Object

The Animation object has a few methods and properties that we can utilize. Some of the ones that will really help fine-tune the animation are speed and delay.

Duration is a Double value that indicates how long should the animation last.

Speed is a Double value, representing a multiplier. This multiplier is used to speed up or slow an animation. A value of say 0.25 is 25%, so a 1 second animation with a speed of 0.25 would last 4 seconds. The lower the number, the slower the animation.

Delay is generally the value that the object needs to wait for before performing the animation.

Types of Animations

There are several types of animations, and when none is specified, SwiftUI uses .default as the choice, which is actually no animation.

The others that we can use to fine-tune our animations are from easeIn, easeOut, easeInOut, linear and spring, interactiveSpring, and interpolatingSpring. Most of these can be called with default duration or be provided a duration in the parameter. The spring animations require a few other parameters or work without as we have used in the preceding code samples.

Paths

Another way to draw shapes is by using an alternative way to draw shapes. This is provided by the Graphics API included in SwiftUI. This involves a series of commands that use absolute positions and points. For all of these points and lines to form a Shape, we use the Path element:

```
Path { path in
    //
}
```

And we can specify the drawing methods inside of the Path closure. The basic commands that we would use with a path to draw the path are move, line, and addLine; these should provide us with the majority of what we are after; to draw curves we also have addQuadCurve, addArc, and addRelativeArc in addition to curve and quadCurve. Lastly, we can also ass other shapes like addEllipse, addRect, addRects, addRoundedRect, and also addPath.

Let's draw a square of 200 x 200. To do that in our path, we need to first move the drawing cursor to the starting point using move; then, we can add a line using the addLine thrice, which will give us the square shape as can be seen in the following code:

```
Path { path in
    path.move(to: CGPoint(x: 10, y: 10))
    path.addLine(to: CGPoint(x: 10, y: 210))
    path.addLine(to: CGPoint(x: 210, y: 210))
    path.addLine(to: CGPoint(x: 210, y: 10))
}
```

If you draw each of the lines if they were commands, you would end up with a U shape, as we did not provide the last line that would close the top of the U and make it a square. The graphics API attempts to close the shape for us, and in this case, it could, so we get a square shape.

Once created, the Path object is also a view, and we can apply most of the modifiers to the Path object as well.

Summary

In this chapter, we learned how to use Timers and act accordingly in the SwiftUI way with minimal code. Next, we learned about the various shapes available and the line styles that can be used to stroke the shapes. Further, we learned about animation and how we can use that in our code. Lastly, we saw how to draw shapes with actual points, line, and curves - that are not provided in the standard shapes and use them in a similar manner as other shapes. In the next chapter, we shall look at the interaction with these elements, namely, using gestures.

CHAPTER 7

Interactive Gestures

So far, we have learned how to use the various UI elements and create interesting UIs. However, these were more or less all simply visual, and in some cases, we added some simple code to start the animation or trigger some event. In this chapter, we shall look at adding interactivity and allowing the code to respond to the user's interactions.

Gestures

Smartphones have touch interfaces, and over the last decade, these touches have been abstracted and become easier to manage and use. The API has classified and categorized some common interaction items into gestures. These gestures include things like tap, longPress, swipe, etc.

To interact with the simulator, we cannot simply use the preview mode; we have to right click the little blue play button to show the context menu from which we select the *Debug Preview* option. This will then allow the interaction and also display the debug statements. Alternatively, we can simply run the code to execute in the simulator.

© Jayant Varma 2019
J. Varma, *SwiftUI for Absolute Beginners*, https://doi.org/10.1007/978-1-4842-5516-2_7

Tap

Let's start with the first basic option available for interactivity. A tap is a gesture that occurs when a user places the finger on the screen and lifts the finger – thereby a tap. SwiftUI has a simple way to access this using the onTapGesture modifier followed by the code we want to run when the tap event occurs in the closure:

```
Text("Hello World!")
.onTapGesture {
    print("Text was tapped")
}
```

In some cases, a tap might not be the right choice, but instead, we might want the user to double tap, that is, tap twice relatively after each other. This is also easily achieved, and we can avail of the count property to set the number of taps to run this closure:

```
Text("Hello World!")
.onTapGesture(count: 2) {
    print("Text was tapped")
}
```

If our code requires to look out for single taps and double taps, we can chain them to have two gesture handlers. Take caution when chaining tap gestures together because the multiple taps greater than two might not work as well.

LongPress

Another gesture option is a longPress gesture, which is *also known as press-and-hold gesture that detects one or more fingers touching the screen for an extended period of time.* The handler already included in SwiftUI is called onLongPressGesture:

```
Text("Hello World!")
.onLongPressGesture {
    print("Text was long pressed")
}
```

This method takes options like minimumDuration, maximumDistance, pressing, and perform, of which perform is the code that we want to perform when this gesture is selected by the user. The minimumDuration is the time the user keeps the finger on the screen, and the maximumDistance is the distance that the user is allowed to slide the finger before it is not considered a long press but a swipe instead. Lastly, pressing is a function that is passed a value which is true at the start of the gesture and false when the gesture is recognized.

Drag

Another simple gesture that many applications employ is a simple drag, which in many simple terms is a swipe. The user places a finger on the screen and then slides the finger to a new location without lifting the finger. This is a swipe and from the UI perspective, a Drag gesture. SwiftUI does not have a simple onDragGesture or an onSwipeGesture as of now. So for gestures like these, we need to use a .gesture modifier and pass it the appropriate Gesture recognizer instead as in the following code:

```
Text("Hello World!")
.gesture(
    DragGesture(minimumDistance: 60)
    .onEnded { drag in
        print(drag)
    }
)
```

The drag parameter passed to the onEnded closure is a structure of DragGesture that contains a timestamp called time, the location where the drag ended in location, the starting location of the drag in startLocation and velocity which will always be 0 in the onEnded closure. However, if we were to have the onChanged closure that would have a similar structure, the velocity would be calculated depending on the start and end location values.

Similarly, swipes can be determined by getting the delta between the start and end locations. The larger value would be the direction of movement, and a negative value on the X-axis would mean a swipe left, and on the Y-axis, it would mean upward swipe.

A good visual way to see this in action is with positioning an element based on the values as can be seen in Figure 7-1:

```
@State private var position: CGPoint = .zero

ZStack {
    Image(systemName: "paperplane")
    .font(.largeTitle)
    .foregroundColor(Color.blue.opacity(0.5))
    .offset(x: self.position.x, y: self.position.y)
    .animation(spring())
    .gesture(DragGesture()
        .onChanged { self.position = $0.location }
    )
}
```

Figure 7-1. *Moving the element by dragging it around the screen*

A little math and a background can make that so much more interesting. We can add a background circle that is the area of where the plane can be dragged, but if it is dragged outside of that area, then it pulls back to the center as seen in Figure 7-2:

```
ZStack {
    Circle()
    .foregroundColor(Color.green.opacity(0.1)
    .frame(width: 320, height: 320)
    Image(systemName: "paperplane")
    .font(.largeTitle)
    .foregroundColor(Color.blue.opacity(0.5))
    .offset(x: self.position.x, y: self.position.y)
    .animation(spring())
    .gesture(DragGesture()
        .onChanged { self.position = $0.location }
        .onEnded { _ in
            if sqrt(self.position.x * self.position.x +
                 self.position.y * self.position.y)
              > 160 {
                self.position = .zero
            }
        }
```

```
            }
        )
    }
```

Figure 7-2. *The Paper plane with the boundary circle*

Rotation

Another gesture that is not uncommon is rotation; this gesture is performed when the user places two fingers on the screen and moves the fingers in a circular motion generally in the same direction. For capturing this gesture, we use the RotationGesture object, and it returns the angle it is currently rotated at on both the onChanged and onEnded closures:

```
@State private var angle = Angle.radians(0)

VStack {
    RoundedRectangle(cornerRadius: 50)
    .foregroundColor(Color.green.opacity(0.1))
    .rotationEffect(angle)
```

```
.gesture( RotationGesture( minimumAngleDelta: Angle.
degrees(1))
.onChanged { angle in
    self.angle = angle
}
onEnded { angle in
    self.angle = Angle.radians(0)
}
}
.padding()
```

Magnification

Another gesture that we can use with SwiftUI is the
MagnificationGesture. This gesture is commonly known as the pinch-
and-zoom gesture. This involves pinching two fingers toward each other
or away to zoom out or in. Setting this up is easy as can be seen in the
following code:

```
struct MagnifyView {
    @State private var scale = 1.0
    var body: some View {
        VStack {
            Image(systemName: "globe")
            .font(.largeTitle)
            .scaleEffect(scale)
            .foregroundColor(Color.black.opacity(0.4))
            .animation(.spring())
            .gesture(MagnificationGesture(
                    minimumScaleDelta: 0.3)
                .onChanges { scale in
                    self.scale = scale
                }
```

```
                .onEnded { scale in
                    self.scale = 0
                }
            )
        }
    }
}
```

We can pinch the globe in the center and zoom in or out, and when we release the gesture, it goes back to the original scale.

Hover

This is a gesture that is unavailable on iOS. However, is available with MacOS and should be available with iPadOS. This is the gesture that is triggered when the mouse cursor is hovered over an element. Since iPadOS supports a mouse and so does macOS, onHover is available for these platforms. Using it is as simple as

```
Text("Hello World")
.onHover(){
    print("Hovering over the element")
}
```

Appearing

While this is not really a gesture, it is an event that is equally important for writing code. We have already seen the use of this early in our chapters where we used it to trigger the animation start. This is similar to the iOS viewDidAppear function where we can write the code that is required to set the view every time it appears on screen:

```
.onAppear {
    print("The view has appeared on screen")
}
```

Disappearing

Similar to the appear function, there is another event available called onDisappear; this is called every time a view is placed off screen or is not displayed. This can be used in tandem with the onAppear where we can set what we need for the code/program to run. Whereas onDisappear is called every time, the view is taken off the screen or another view becomes the foreground view.

Combinations

As stressed numerous times earlier, the whole idea with SwiftUI was to allow for composition and to allow for combining items and creating more complex items from it. In some terms, it's the developer's version of Minecraft; we can take the items and put them together to form more advanced items. It may not be such an apt analogy, but it should convey the point that it is composable and powerful.

There are some functions that allow us to work with gestures including SimultaneousGesture, HighPriorityGesture, SequenceGesture, and ExclusiveGesture.

Summary

In this chapter, we looked at using gestures and events to make the code interactive. We also looked at the various gestures and how we could chain them or use them together or separately as the case may be. In the next chapter, we shall explore the new feature – "Previews."

CHAPTER 8

Previews

In the last chapter, we learned about gestures, and throughout the chapters, we have been looking at and taking advantage of one new feature called Previews. These let us preview the UI without having to run the application, and with Live Previews, we can even interact with the UI without having to run it. In this chapter, we shall look deeper into this functionality and see how we can take advantage of it to our benefit.

Preview

One of the things that we are so used to these days came with a very strange acronym; it used to be called WYSIWYG, pronounced as wisi-wig. It stands for What You See Is What You Get. This became popular with the days of Disk Operating System with software like WordStar, which many would not have even heard of. Users would type out letters and have no idea on how it looked until they printed it out; with *wysiwyg*, it allowed the users to preview what it looked like prior to printing. This then went on to become the graphical user interface–based desktop publishing, and now, many applications use this out of the box without even calling it *wysiwyg*. It's just present. However, when developing especially with respect to creating UIs, developers still do not have a simpler workflow; they need to compile and upload the UI to a simulator or device before they can see the UI. This was a big issue that slowed the pace of development.

© Jayant Varma 2019
J. Varma, *SwiftUI for Absolute Beginners*, https://doi.org/10.1007/978-1-4842-5516-2_8

The developers at Apple, especially the team that works on the development tools, keep looking trying to push the envelope and add new functionality to make Xcode a better integrated development environment (IDE). This year in 2019, they released SwiftUI, and with it, they also introduced a new functionality called *Preview*.

What this does is that it creates a snippet of code and then compiles it and runs it; the resulting UI is then displayed in Xcode itself. So, we get a preview of what we are creating and change some text or tweak a value, and it updates instantaneously. Changes that affect the logic or change the execution of the application can require pressing the Resume option as Xcode pauses the preview. We can see the preview in Figure 8-1.

Figure 8-1. *Xcode showing a Preview for the code*

The Advantage

While we know that Interface Builder allows us to create interfaces visually so we already have an idea of what it would look like, when we want to fine-tune our UI, look at how the interface might look with different colors and fonts or, even now with the new dark and light mode settings, how it would look in either; UI Builder can only help so much. Another thing that makes previews more useful is that we can now see the UI with our data rather than just the placeholders that we use while designing the UI.

How Does It Work?

When we enable previews, Xcode builds the code we have written, runs it, and then displays the results to us. It does this intelligently; Xcode knows what file or view it is that we have altered and compiles just that file or view accordingly. It then injects that compiled code into the application using Swift's dynamic replacement feature. Since the amount of code that needs to be compiled is significantly smaller, this keeps on happening with every small change that we make. This ensures that the feedback on the changes is much quicker. For a lot of things like strings or numbers, it does not even need to be recompiled. The new values are simply injected into the application to provide an instant feedback. This is not how Xcode thinks the view will look like as we get with building an UI; this is actually how it will look because Xcode is running the code to generate this view. All of the custom assets, custom logic, and everything that we would get only at runtime are available and can be seen in the preview. Additional things like access to UserDefaults for example are also available to use in *previews*.

Architecture

While Apple stayed with the MVC architecture for a very long time, it was time to move and adopt some of the other architectures that were available. There are pros and cons of each of the architectures; however with the SwiftUI and Combine binding patterns, it seems that Apple has moved to the MVVM and Reactive type architecture. With previews and composition, the MVVM pattern makes most sense where we can have a View Model that can help render the previews and can also be tested independent of the view.

We can create a *ViewModel* from the Model containing just the data that we want to present, and this can be tested until we get it right. Then this is presented to the user or rendered in previews. That can be also considered as the Model View Presenter design pattern.

Let us create our *ViewModel* to hold and display a single dessert:

```
struct DessertViewModel: Codable, Identifiable {
    let id = UUID()
    var name: String
    var image: String
    var ratings: Int
}
```

And we will create a single entry for us that can allow us to use a single dessert for previews called icecream:

```
extension DessertViewModel {
    static var icecream: DessertViewModel {
        return DessertViewModel(name: "Ice Cream",
                    image: "TurtlePumpkinIcecream",
                ratings: 3)
    }
}
```

Now, we have a *ViewModel*, and we can get the `icecream` item by referring to it as `DessertViewModel.icecream`.

What to Preview

Xcode would generally not know what to preview. The way to let Xcode know what it is that we want it to preview is by using the `PreviewProvider` protocol. When we create a new SwiftUI file, it creates a structure for the View and also the structure for the Preview. That looks something like this and would render as can be seen in Figure 8-2:

```
struct DessertViewPreview: PreviewProvider {
    static var previews: some View {
        DessertView(.icecream)
    }
}
```

This would create a preview for our `DessertView` which would display information regarding an `icecream`. This is the content, just like the content that we have been adding to our SwiftUI views that we have been creating so far. This code lives as part of the SwiftUI file; it is also compiled alongside the rest of the application code. Therefore, we can also use custom logic, assets, and so on, including data from other classes:

```
struct DessertView: View {
    let model: DessertViewModel

    var body: some View {
        HStack{
            Text("\(model.image)")
            VStack {
                Text("\(model.name)")
                Text("\(model.ratings)")
            }
```

125

```
        }
    }
}
```

Figure 8-2. *The preview of the basic* `DessertViewModel`

The other advantage of previews is that it lives in the same file and is in text format, so it can be checked in with the rest of the code and shared with the team. This also allows everyone that can check out the code to see how the code would render. Even as our code changes and evolves, the previews stay in sync.

Customizing Previews

Whenever we invoke the preview, the preview uses the device that is set for the Run Destination in the active scheme, generally seen on the top of the IDE near the Run button. If we wanted to change the device and preview it in another device, we could change the device in the scheme, but that is tedious. So, we have an easier way to manage this; we can use the `previewDevice` modifier and pass it the name of the device as seen in the Active Scheme:

```
struct DessertViewPreview: PreviewProvider {
    static var previews: some View {
        DessertView(.icecream)
        .previewDevice("iPhone SE")
    }
}
```

If we wanted to preview this for two different devices, then we can do that too simply by creating a `Group` and adding another instance and provide another `previewDevice` to it as follows:

```
struct DessertViewPreview: PreviewProvider {
    static var previews: some View {
        Group {
            DessertView(.icecream)
            .previewDevice("iPhone SE")
            DessertView(.icecream)
            .previewDevice("iPhone XS")
        }
    }
}
```

And now, we have two different devices showing us how the app would look on them as seen in Figure 8-3.

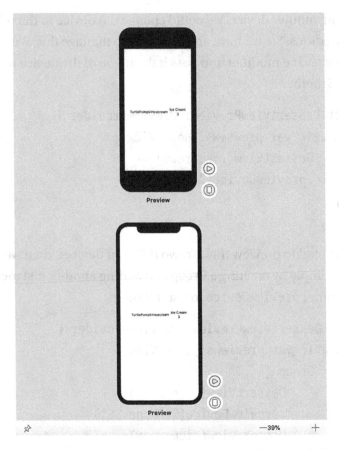

Figure 8-3. *Preview showing the same element for two different devices*

Preview: Just the View

While it is neat to see the whole device in the preview, sometimes all that we might be interested in is previewing just that view as it is. It could be as small as a Label or a tableView cell. Xcode provides us with another modifier called previewLayout. The previewLayout has three options; the first is the device that takes the current device as the preview device.

The next is a fixed size, provided via a width and height. The last option is sizeThatFits which displays the contents in the smallest size that is required to contain the view:

```
Group {
    DessertView(.icecream)
    .previewLayout(.device)

    DessertView(.icecream)
    .previewLayout(.sizeThatFits)

    DessertView(.icecream)
    .previewLayout(.fixed(width: 200, height: 200))
}
```

Since the preview's API is part of the SwiftUI, we can take advantage of this fact when we write our previews. We can use the environment modifier .environment; it takes two parameters – a keypath and a value. Using this, we can quickly and easily preview how the view will look with the modified values, such as sizeCategory where we can specify like extraLarge, large, small, and so on.

When we have multiple previews, it is difficult to distinguish between the various previews. There is another modifier that allows us to be able to easily distinguish between the previews by providing it a name using the previewDisplayName modifier as can be seen in Figure 8-4.

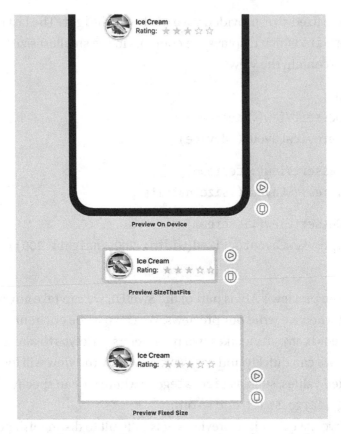

Figure 8-4. *Display the different preview layouts with their captions*

Note   We can have a maximum of 15 previews.

Using Assets in Preview

While using previews, we can provide data, and so on. to the preview. However, in cases of images, we could add temporary placeholder images that are used for displaying in previews, but then these images could get compiled into the binary. All of those would increase the size unnecessarily. Now, Xcode has a new feature that allows us to add developmental assets. When we create a new project, it is automatically created for us and can be found under the "**Preview Content**" group in the project files. We can also create a new .xcassets file and add it to the project via the project settings to be included for Preview only under Development Assets, as seen in Figure 8-5.

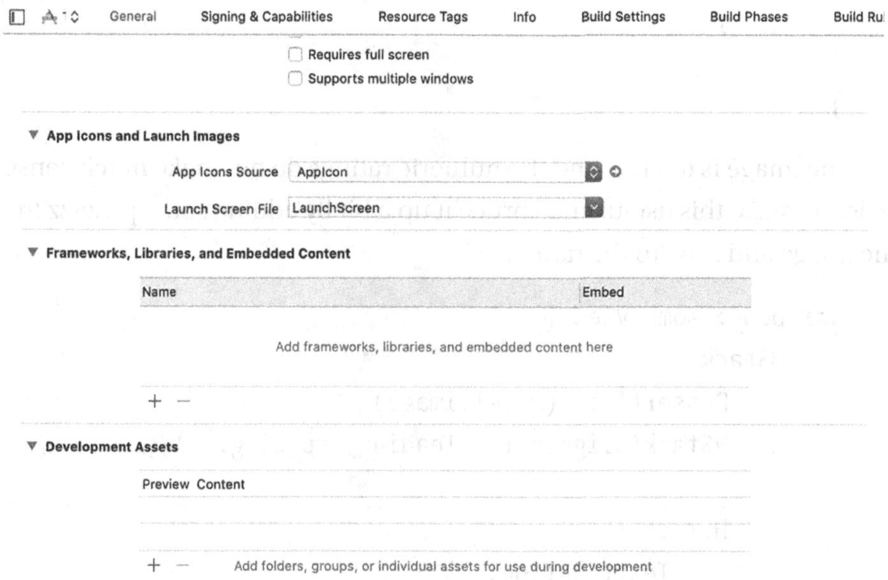

Figure 8-5. *The Project settings to add under Development Assets*

Now that we can add images to our preview for development mode alone, let us use them in our DessertView. First, we change the Text to an Image so that it can display the image:

```
struct DessertView: View {
    let model: DessertViewModel
```

```
    var body: some View {
        HStack{
            Image("\(model.image)")
            VStack {
                Text("\(model.name)")
                Text("\(model.ratings)")
            }
        }
    }
```

The image is too big, and the numeric ratings do not make much sense, so let us make this useful and spruce it up a bit by adding some pizzazz to the image and stars to the rating:

```
var body: some View {
    HStack {
        DessertImage(model.image)
        VStack(alignment: .leading, spacing: 0) {
        ...
        HStack {
            Text("Rating: ")
            ForEach(0..<model.ratings) { _ in
                Image(systemName: "star.fill")
                .foregroundColor(Color.yellow)
            }
            ForEach(model.ratings..<5) { _ in
                Image(systemName: "star")
                .foregroundColor(Color.gray.opacity(0.5))
            }
        }
        ...
```

```
            }
        }
    }
```

With the Image, we clip the shape and apply some border and shadow. The problem with developers calling MVC as Massive View Controllers was because a lot of code was dumped into the view controllers, and we are kind of ending up with the same if we try to make our image look pretty as per the design. We can abstract that code into a separate function, and that way, the code lengths would still remain manageable. So, we create a function DessertImage and pass it the model.image so that it can display the image:

```swift
func DessertImage(_ image: String) -> some View {
    return Image(image)
    .resizable()
    .clipShape(Circle())
    .overlay(Circle().stroke(Color.white, lineWidth: 2))
    .padding(2)
    .overlay(Circle().stroke(Color.black.opacity(0.1)))
    .shadow(radius: 3)
    .padding(4)
    .frame(width: 72, height: 72)
}
```

And we have a lovely looking DessertView single item. This is closer to what it could look in our final application as can be seen in Figure 8-6.

Figure 8-6. *The DessertView single item as required at runtime*

Making It Useful

Now that we have been able to preview the DessertView single item
icecream, how would it look when we had our application running with
multiple items? So, we can add multiple entries for icecream to simulate
rows, after all that is how we are used to creating tableViews in *UI Builder*.
So, we will create a ListView that will display our items in a list so that we
can add multiple entries as it will look when the application is run:

```
struct DessertListView: View {
    let desserts: [DessertViewModel]

    var body: some View {
        NavigationView {
            List {
                ForEach(desserts) { dessert in
                    DessertView(model: dessert)
                }
            }
            .navigationBarTitle("Just Desserts")
        }
    }
}
```

And now in the preview, we can now pass it the desserts as

```
struct DessertList_Previews: PreviewProvider {
    static var previews: some View {
        DessertList(desserts:[.icecream, .icecream, .icecream])
    }
}
```

Figure 8-7. The List of items repeating in preview

This creates the list with the repeating elements of icecream as can be seen in Figure 8-7.

Adding Sample Data

With the method discussed earlier, we see three items in the list, but that is not very useful. We are simply seeing the same item; it does not give us a representation of what the application would look like at runtime. We could pass it some dummy data from a JavaScript Object Notation (JSON) file:

```
extension DessertList_Previews {
  static var sampleDesserts: [DessertViewModel] {
    guard let url = Bundle.main.url(forResource:
            "SampleDesserts", withExtension: "json"),
          let data = try? Data(contentOf: url)
    else { return [] }
    let decoder = JSONDecoder()
    let array = try? decoder.decode([DessertViewModel].self,
              from: data)
    return array ?? [.icecream]
  }
}
```

In the preceding code, we parse the JSON that is locally saved in *Preview Content* called SampleDesserts.json, and this is then made available via a property called sampleDesserts that we can simply use as

```
struct DessertList_Previews: PreviewProvider {
  static var previews: some View {
    DessertList(sampleDesserts)
  }
}
```

And we shall see the sample data populate the list now instead of repeating three icecreams as seen in Figure 8-8.

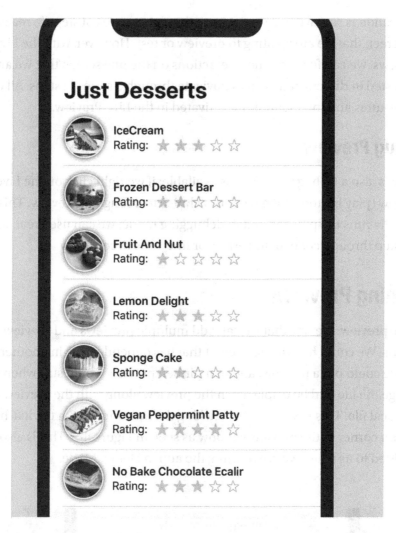

Figure 8-8. *The sample data populating the list view*

Live Preview

If previews have made an impact as something amazing, Live Previews
are even more amazing. When the code is run in a Live Preview, it is
interactive, that is, we can interact with the preview as if it was run
on a simulator. The difference again is that in the simulator when the

application is run, we have to navigate through a series of steps to reach the screen that we are wanting to preview or test. However, with the Live Previews, we can focus on the interactions on the one screen that we are interested in directly rather than navigate through a series of steps. All of the gestures and interactions are activated in the Live Preview.

Debug Preview

There is also a Debug mode that is available; if we right click on the Live Preview (play button), then it offers a choice to debug the preview. This basically runs the preview, but in debugging mode, we can use breakpoints and step through code to find errors or fine-tune accordingly.

Pinning Previews

In the preview, we saw that we can add multiple previews and preview layouts. We could have a component that has dependencies in another file; we could pin a preview, and that pinned preview would stay when we change the file and be displayed in the preview along with the preview of that local file. This is achieved by clicking the little pin icon at the left-hand bottom corner of the preview window as seen in Figure 8-9. This is also provided to us when we are running the app in Debug Mode.

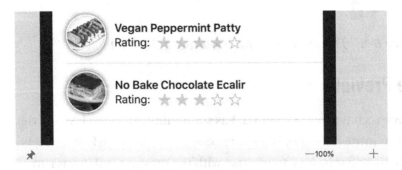

Figure 8-9. *The pin icon to pin a specific preview*

Summary

In this chapter, we learned a fair few things; the most important of all is that we can visually see what our UI would look like while developing and not having to run the application to check that. We can also pass it some test data to populate and view what the UI would look like. We also learned about using View Models, though there is more, and this is by no means the best practice in using any of the design patterns as this is attempting to demonstrate how to use previews. In the next chapter, we shall look at integrating UIKit with SwiftUI and vice versa.

CHAPTER 9

Integrating UIKit

In the previous chapter, we learned about Previews and how we can view our UI while we are still developing the SwiftUI code. This allows us to view the layout, and if we are in debugging mode, we can also interact with our UI. So far, we have kept our SwiftUI separate and not used any UIKit either. It is almost as if this were a separate technology or language.

In this chapter, we shall go a little further and look at how we can integrate our SwiftUI and UIKit elements together.

SwiftUI

When we create a SwiftUI project, there are a couple of files that are created for us. Like any other Swift applications so far, we see an `AppDelegate.swift`. This file allows us to add code to manage remote notifications, and so on. This is the first point in the lifecycle of the application. For a SwiftUI application, it returns a default `UISceneConfiguration` for the `application(_:configurationForConnecting:options:)` function and looks like

```
return UISceneConfiguration(name: "Default Configuration",
sessionRole: connectingSceneSession.role)
```

The next file is `SceneDelegate.swift,` and this is the file that is defined as

```
Class SceneDelegate: UIResponder, UIWindowSceneDelegate {
```

© Jayant Varma 2019
J. Varma, *SwiftUI for Absolute Beginners*, https://doi.org/10.1007/978-1-4842-5516-2_9

It has a function called scene that is defined as follows:

```
func scene(_ scene: UIScene, willConnectTo session:
            UISceneSession,
        options connectionOptions:
            UIScene.ConnectionOptions) {
    if let windowScene = scene as? UIWindowScene {
        let window = UIWindow(windowScene: windowScene)
        window.rootViewController =
            UIHostingController(rootView: MyFirstApp())
        self.window = window
        window.makeKeyAndVisible()
    }
}
```

In this little block of code, the only line that is of importance is the one that sets the rootViewController. We are aware from developing for iOS using Swift or Objective-C that the rootViewController is the main view that is visible underneath, the first view so as to say. We can change this to swap out views. This preceding code block sets the SwiftUI structure that we create as the root view. So, it will display that for us.

Note   For a non-SwiftUI project, this scene function is much simpler and looks like guard let _ = (scene as? UIWindowScene) else { return }.

And the third piece of the puzzle that makes this all work is the Info. plist file. There is a new entry here, which is called Application Scene Manifest. This looks something like

▼ UIApplicationSceneManifest
    UIApplicationSupportsMultipleScenes

▼ UISceneConfigurations
   ▼ UIWindowsSceneSessionRoleApplication
      ▼ Item 0 (Default Configuration)
         UISceneConfigurationName
         UISceneDelegateClassName
         UILaunchStoryboardName

The UISceneDelegateClassName is set here which looks like $(PRODUCT_MODULE_NAME).SceneDelegate; this is what directs the code to run the SceneDelegate.swift. The UISceneConfigurationName is the "Default Configuration" as was set in the AppDelegates application function.

Another important thing to see there is the same line that uses a function called UIHostingController. This is the bit that we shall use in this chapter to integrate SwiftUI and UIKit.

Now that we know the few basics that make the project use and work with SwiftUI from a blank project, let us look into this further.

Integrating SwiftUI into UIKit

We can start a non-SwiftUI project which will simply run when we choose compile and run as we have been used to developing with Swift. Next, we create a new SwiftUI file; this shall hold our Custom UI, and we call it CustomUIChild (we can call it whatever we want, but for the purposes of this example, it is called so). When Xcode creates a new template, it creates the body with a single Text element with the text *Hello World!*; for now we'll leave it at that because the idea here is to integrate the SwiftUI view into our regular UIKit application view.

In our project hierarchy, we see a file called `ViewController.swift` where the code for our view controller is added. Let's modify the `viewDidLoad` function to include the SwiftUI view:

```
let sUIView = UIHostingController(rootView: CustomUIChild)
    sUIView.view.translatesAutoresizingMaskIntoConstraints =
    false
    sUIView.view.frame = self.view.bounds
    self.addChild(sUIView)
    self.view.addSubview(sUIView.view)
```

Let's see what is happening in the preceding code. The first line creates an instance of the `UIHostingController` with the `rootView` as the `CustomUIChild` struct that we created in SwiftUI. This is what we saw earlier happens in the `SceneDelegate.swift` file for our SwiftUI projects.

The next line sets the `translateAutoresizingMaskIntoConstraints` to `false` which basically disallows the autoresizing mask to be translated into AutoLayout constraints. By setting it to `false`, we ask AutoLayout to dynamically calculate the size and position of the view. Creating an UI element from storyboard also sets this property to `false`.

Next, we set the frame to be that of the main view, that is, fill the entire space.

Then, we add the child to the hierarchy and set a parent-child relationship between the view and the SwiftUI view.

Lastly, we add the view of our SwiftUI view to the view hierarchy so that it is now visible on the screen.

Integrating UIKit into SwiftUI

The same way around, we can also embed an UIKit element into the SwiftUI view hierarchy. The way to do that is by using the `UIViewRepresentable` or the `UIViewControllerRepresentable`.

With SwiftUI, the simplest view requires a render and maybe a state as well; this involves adding two functions makeUIView and updateUIView. We need to create a representable SwiftUI view and add the two functions. For this example, let us add a new element in Swift UI, a MapView. First, we need to import the libraries that we need, namely, UIKit and MapKit:

```
import UIKit
import MapKit

struct MapView: UIViewRepresentable {
  typealias MyContext = UIViewRepresentableContext <MapView>
    func makeUIView(context: MapView) -> MKMapView {
      return MKMapView(frame: .zero)
    }

    func updateUIView(_ view: MKMapView, context: MapView) {
      let coordinate = CLLocationCoordinate2D(
          latitude: -37.8177131, longitude: 144.9679939)
      let span = MKCoordinateSpan(latitudeDelta: 0.05,
          longitudeDelta: 0.05)
      let region = MKCoordinateRegion(center: coordinate,
          span: span)
      view.setRegion(region, animated: true)
    }
}
```

We can now add this MapView like any other SwiftUI Element in the body, like

```
var body: some View {
    VStack {
        MapView()
    }
}
```

And we get a Map showing Melbourne as seen in Figure 9-1 (though the preview will not show anything, we need to run it in either the simulator or in Live Preview mode).

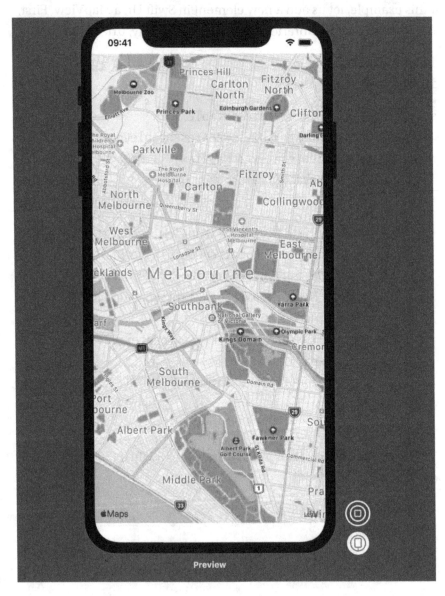

Figure 9-1. *Custom MapView element from UIKit*

This custom control would always show us Melbourne as the coordinates are set for Melbourne. We could also pass the coordinates on initializing the control with a few modifications where it could access the date from the passed data. Generally, with the Swift classes or object-oriented programming, we can pass the data to the initializers, and it can set the data. However, with SwiftUI, there are some limitations that do not allow us to use this functionality. The main reason for that is the passed parameters are normal data whereas SwiftUI uses State or Binding type variables. To that, we have to work with only these data types. Let us look at the modifications that allow us to send custom coordinates to the MapView we created:

```
struct MyMapView: View {
    @State private var coords = CLLocationCoordinate2D
    (latitude: -37.8177131, longitude: 144.9679939)

    var body: some View {
        VStack {
            MapView(coords: $coords)
        }
    }
}
```

In our MapView declaration, we need to make some changes that can now accept these custom coordinates instead of the hard-coded values we had earlier:

```
struct MapView: UIViewRepresentable {
    @Binding var coords: CLLocationCoordinate2D

    typealias MyContext = UIViewRepresentableContext <MapView>
    func makeUIView(context: MapView) -> MKMapView {
        return MKMapView(frame: .zero)
    }
```

```
func updateUIView(_ view: MKMapView, context: MapView) {
  let coordinate = CLLocationCoordinate2D(
    //  latitude: -37.8177131, longitude: 144.9679939)
    latitude: coords.latitude, longitude: coords.
    longitude)
  let span = MKCoordinateSpan(latitudeDelta: 0.05,
      longitudeDelta: 0.05)
  let region = MKCoordinateRegion(center: coordinate,
      span: span)
  view.setRegion(region, animated: true)
  }
}
```

We shall still see MapView displaying Melbourne because the coordinates are still for Melbourne. We can pass other values and see it will update accordingly.

One thing to note is that we used a State and Binding variable where we made the State variable private and not the Binding variable. If we made that private, then we would not be able to access it, and the compiler would complain that it is not set.

Passing Parameters

While the preceding code works fine, there can be times when we would rather pass the data to the element, rather than simply have it hard coded in the calling view or the subview. In our case, we would have called it as MapView(latitude: <VALUE>, longitude: <VALUE>). However, if we tried that, it does not work very well. The solution is to convert the values into a State or Binding value accordingly:

```
struct Balance: View {
    @Binding var amount: Double
```

```
    var body: some View {
        HStack {
            Image(systemName: "person.crop.rectangle.fill")
            Text("Balance : $\(amount)")
        }
    }
}
```

Then, when we use it say like

```
struct ShowBalance: View {
    ...
    var body: some View {
        Balance()
    }
    ...
}
```

Note   Apple suggests that we use a `Binding` to provide a state that is not local to the view.

This does not work, and the compiler complains as it needs us to pass a value for amount in the ShowBalance definition. So, we change it to

```
var body: some View {
    Balance(amount: 1234.56)
}
```

This will still complain as it cannot assign a value of type `Double` to expected argument type `Binding<Double>`. The first thing we can do is create a `State` variable that we can pass to this:

```
@State private var amount: Double

var body: some View {
    Balance(amount: $amount)
}
```

But now, the preview would not work with this declaration, since now `ShowBalance()` requires the `amount` to be set. In addition to that, since the declaration for this variable is `private`, we cannot access it from outside of this structure declaration nor use the member-wise initializer that we get with a structure.

So, what do we do? How can we resolve this issue? The lack of documentation and the unavailability of information covering this topic can be limiting. This is because these are still changing.

Casting Values

The issues that we just saw are genuine, and there will always be the need to pass data from one structure to another. If we try to modify a state variable value from outside the body, we get an error. Plus, we made our Binding variable public; what we might need for true abstraction is making it private. How do we deal with this? How do we pass values – the solution here is casting values:

```
struct Balance: View {
    @Binding private var amount: Double

    init(_ amount: Binding<Double>) {
        self._amount = amount
    }
```

```
var body: some View {
    HStack {
        Image(systemName: "person.crop.rectangle.fill")
        Text("Balance: $\(amount)")
    }
}
}
```

The thing to note in the preceding code is that we have an initializer that gets passed a value of type Binding<Double>, not a Double. And another thing that might be different than what we have seen so far is the self._amount = amount. When we declare a Binding or a State, it creates a couple of variables and the code looks like the following:

```
@State var amount: Double
```

This preceding line gets translated to the following code:

```
private var _amount: State<Double> = State(initialValue: 0.0)
private var $amount: Binding<Double> {
                    return _amount.projectedValue
        }
private var amount: Double{
    get { return _amount.value }
    nonmutating set { _amount.value = newValue }
}
```

Earlier, we saw that we could use the $variable to provide a version that can be modified. Similarly, we can use the _variable to assign the values of a Binding type.

Now, we need to make the changes to the ShowBalance declaration as

```
struct ShowBalance: View {
    @State private var amount: Double

    init(_ amount: Double = 0.0) {
        self._amount = State(initialValue: amount)
    }

    var body: some View {
        VStack {
            BankView($amount)
                .font(.largeTitle)
        }
    }
}
```

Here, we have an initializer that takes a Double value and sets the value to the state variable by using the initialValue parameter. So, now in the preview, we can pass a value like we do with other Elements, say Text("Hello World!"):

```
struct ShowBalance_Previews: PreviewProvider {
    static var previews: some View {
        ShowBalance(1234.56)
    }
}
```

Since we use the default value in the initializer, if we call it without any value, simply as ShowBalance(), then it is initialized with a default value of 0.0.

Summary

This feature is still being developed, and there isn't a lot of documentation around this topic. Nevertheless, the way to manage this is using either of State, Binding, Observable, ObservedObject, Environment, and the like. At all times, the principle of Single Source of Truth must be followed, which means the data can flow from an object to the other. If required, we can transform the data into the format that we need, either a State or Binding. We are nearly at the end of our journey in beginning to develop with SwiftUI. In the next chapter, we shall look at some tips and tricks with SwiftUI.

CHAPTER 10

Accessing API Data

In the previous chapter, we learned about Previews and how we can see
the UI and even interact with it. In this chapter, we shall have a look at
downloading data from an API and decode the JSON data.

REST API Data

The most common way to get data from an API is using an `URLSession`. It
involves a couple of steps, like in the following code:

1. Create the URL.

2. Start a `dataTask`.

3. Write the completion handler for the task.

4. Convert the data into a format.

5. Display the data.

```
let url = "https://icanhazdadjoke.com/"
URLSession.shared.dataTask(with: url) {
    data, response, error in
    if let data = data,
        let httpResponse = response as? HTTPURLResponse,
        (200..<300) ~= httpResponse.statusCode,
        let strData = String(bytes: data, encoding: .utf8)
```

© Jayant Varma 2019
J. Varma, *SwiftUI for Absolute Beginners*, https://doi.org/10.1007/978-1-4842-5516-2_10

```
    {
        print(strData)
    }

}.resume()
```

This piece of code can download the data from the web site and print it in the console. The only thing is that by default, this API returns an entire web page (HTML), so parsing it can become really daunting.

Getting Text Data

If we look at the web site under the API section, it tells us about the way we can get the joke as text or as JSON; for this, we need to specify this in the headers. To get the plain text, we need the text/plain, and for the JSON format, we need to specify the application/JSON. However, when we use the dataTask with an URL, we cannot add headers. Instead, we use dataTask with the urlRequest as it allows us to set the Headers as

```
let url = "https://icanhazdadjoke.com/"
var urlRequest = URLRequest(url: url)
urlRequest.addValue("text/plain",
        forHTTPHeaderField: "Accept")
URLSession.shared.dataTask(with: urlRequest) {
    data, response, error in
    if let data = data,
        let httpResponse = response as? HTTPURLResponse,
        (200..<300) ~= httpResponse.statusCode,
        let strData = String(bytes: data, encoding: .utf8)
    {
        print(strData)
    }

}.resume()
```

Getting JSON Data

In the same way as we got the joke in text format, we can get the same in JSON format. For consuming any data in JSON format, we need to first create a structure to hold the data, and secondly, we need to make it conform to the Codable protocol. If we check the API section, we see that the JSON data looks something like

```
{
"id":"R7UfaahVfFd",
"joke":"Where do hamburgers go to dance? The meat-ball",
"status":200
}
```

With this information, we can declare our structure as

```
struct Joke: Codable {
    var id: String
    var joke: String
    var status: Int
}
```

In the line where we convert the Data into a String, we try to decode the data into JSON in the Joke structure format, just after we get the data from the urlSession:

```
...
let json = try? JSONDecoder().decode(Joke.self, from: data) {
  print(json)
}
```

Combine to the Rescue

Throughout the book, we have looked at a single theme that has been dominant; the direction that Apple is offering developers is a composable and easy-to-use interface. Similarly, why should getting REST API data asynchronously be any different? We already know the steps, so why can we not chain them together to make it readable and easy to use?

```swift
func getJoke() {
    let url = URL(string: "https://icanhazdadjoke.com/")!
    var urlRequest = URLRequest(url: url)
    urlRequest.addValue("text/plain",
               forHTTPHeaderField: "Accept")
    let request = URLSession.shared.dataTaskPublisher
    (for: urlRequest)
    .map { $0.data }
    .replaceError(with: nil)
    .eraseToAnyPublisher()
    .receive(on: DispatchQueue.main)
    .sink(receiveValue: { joke in
      if let joke = joke,
         let strJoke = String(bytes: joke, encoding: .utf8) {
         print("\(strJoke)")
      }
    })
}
```

Here's quite a bit that we would look into as these are quite new, and we haven't seen these as yet. The first is that we create a new Publisher from the dataTask; we looked at Publishers briefly in Chapter 4.

This creates a publisher which publishes data received from the provided urlRequest. Now starts the interesting aspects of composition using combine.

The next thing we do is transform the data using map. The data format from `dataTaskPublisher` returns a `data`, `response,` and `error`. We are interested only in the data portion, so we return the data in the `map` function using `.map {$0.data}`.

Next, we use the `replaceError(with: nil)` to change the error (if any) to `nil`, that is, discard the error when it occurs.

We looked at `some` keywords in Chapter 3 which was the opposite of Generics, that is, it removes the specific information and makes it generic. Similarly, `.eraseToAnyPublisher()` removes the information from the publisher to make it a cleaner generic one; as with the chaining, there is a whole lot of information associated with this publisher at the end of the chaining. This generally is at the end of the chain.

Then, we set the `.receive(on: DispatchQueue.main)`; this defines the scheduler that would receive the published events. This can be a `RunLoop.main`, a `DispatchQueue.main,` or an `OperationQueue`.

Lastly, we also subscribe to the events using `.sink` this takes closures for `receiveCompletion` and `receiveValue`. In our preceding example, we are only using the `receiveValue` closure because we do not care much about the completion or error at this point, more so because we replaced the error with `nil`. If we were to also handle the `receiveCompletion`, we would get either a `finished` or a `failure` which contains the `error`.

We received our joke as `Data,` and we convert that into `String` format for being able to read it as text.

Using JSON Data

In this example, we are receiving the joke in plain text, say we up the ante and want to consume JSON data. We already have the `Joke` structure defined earlier and also are aware that we need to send the `application/JSON` in the header. However, earlier when we got the data, we converted the data into a `Joke` structure by Decoding it. Similarly, in this case too, we need to decode the JSON into a Joke structure. We can do that in the same way of chaining our functions using a .decode just before we use the type erasure and replace the error with nil:

```
.decode(type: Joke.self, decoder: JSONDecoder())
```

Joke App

Let us now use this information and connect it to an App UI so that we can see the jokes in a table view, we can press a button to get another joke, and we can see these jokes in a list.

Getting a Joke

We can create a function that will download a joke for us from the web site. However, we saw that in SwiftUI, the UI needs to be rendered when a state changes. This was possible with the bindings that were created by @State and @Binding Property Wrappers. So first, we need a @State property wrapper that holds the jokes as an array:

```
@State private var jokes:[Joke] = []
```

We could have made this into an array of strings, but SwiftUI has some requirements that need the items in a loop using ForEach that has to conform to Identifiable. We could create our own structure that has an id, thereby conforming to the Identifiable protocol. However, the JSON provides us with an id that suffices as an identifier.

Note   If we do not use this, and instead use a numeric range, there are instances where the UI elements do not render; now, this is unclear if that is a bug or intentional. The debug output does let us know that there was no identifier. This could be a beta thing or a bug; hopefully, it will be resolved in future versions of SwiftUI.

We write the function to get the following joke and append the joke into the array:

```
func getJoke() {
    var urlRequest = URLRequest(url: url)
    urlRequest.addValue("application/json",
                    forHTTPHeaderField: "Accept")
    let cancellable = URLSession.shared.dataTaskPublisher(
                    for: urlRequest)
    .map { $0.data }
    .decode(type: Joke.selfm decoder: JSONDecoder())
    .replaceError(with: Joke(id:"---", joke: "Not found",
                    status: 404)
    .eraseToAnyPublisher()
    .receive(on: DispatchQueue.main)
    .sink(receiveValue: { joke in
        self.jokes.insert(joke, at: 0)
    })
}
```

Note   We used the *insert* to add items into the joke array instead of using *append*. We did so because we want the latest joke to be on the top; if we used *append*, it would have added the newer joke at the end of the array.

Displaying the Jokes

Now comes the interesting part to display the jokes; the beauty is that it can be achieved in many ways; however, the easiest way and consistent way that we could use is a TableView or a List as it is known in SwiftUI. We can do so by replacing the following code for the body:

```
var body: some View {
    NavigationView {
        VStack {
            List {
                ForEach(self.jokes( { joke in
                    Text(joke.joke)
                })
            }
            .navigationBarTitle(Text("ICanHazDadJokes"))
            Button(action: {self.getJoke()},
                    Label: {Text("Get Another Joke")}
        }
    }
    .onAppear(perform: { self.getJoke() })
}
```

The glue that binds all of this together is the SwifUI bindings that we have yet to declare, which comes in the form of a @State variable which is declared just before the body declaration as

```
@State private var jokes: [Joke] = []
```

How it all functions is that when the body is rendered the first time, it triggers the self.getJoke() function that is declared under onAppear. As soon as the function is called, it will get a joke and add it into the self.jokes array. Since this is a state variable and will cause the body to be re-rendered each time its value changes, this insertion of value triggers the body to be rendered, thereby adding a new row in the tableview with the new joke.

There we have it, an easy-to-build and easy-to-use DadJokes app as seen in Figure 10-1.

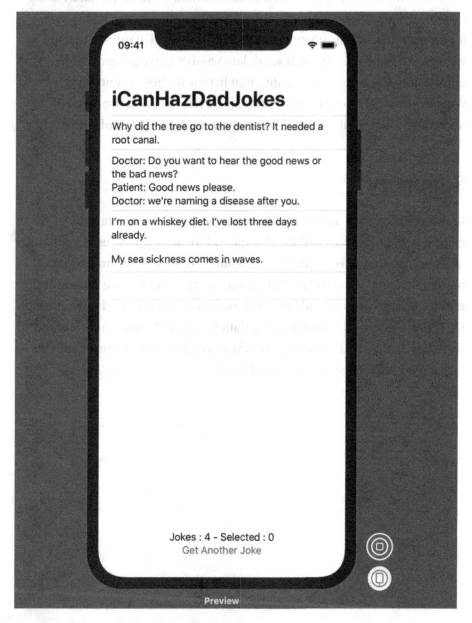

Figure 10-1. *The DadJokes app running showing some jokes*

Using Combine

There is another way to get online data streamed to the application using Combine. We shall not delve into that methodology in detail. However, for an overview of how it works, we looked at this in Chapter 4, where we create a Publisher that will send data whenever we get any. In the application, we set up a subscriber that listens to these events, and whenever we get one, we extract/transform the data and use/update accordingly, something similar to how we used the timer publisher.

Summary

In this chapter, we learned the difference between the regular way of getting data from a REST API endpoint and the new way to use Combine and composition. It is straightforward and simple and also makes for readability; one can see at a single glance what is happening rather than trying to wade through and figure out nested conditions and unwrapping ifs. We also learned how to bind the data from an API to include it with the UI and make it all seamless. This keeps in line with the principles we learned about "The single Source of Truth."

CHAPTER 11

Tips and Tricks

In the last chapter, we had a look at accessing data from REST API. We are now at the end of our journey on beginning development with SwiftUI. We have learned all about the various UI elements and learned to wrap elements from UIKit into SwiftUI and vice versa. In this chapter, we shall look at some little tips and tricks to maximize the utilization of utilize SwiftUI in making apps.

Rendering Elements

The first tip and most important to remember that every time a @State variable is altered, the body is re-rendered. Unless we are after a Disco Ball effect, we need to be careful about applying a background color at random than from a model. The following example outlines this issue better:

```
let colors:[Color] = [.red, .green, .blue, .orange,
.purple, .gray]
let timer = Timer.publish(every: 0.5, on: .current, in:
.common).autoconnect()

struct MyColoredLabel: View {
    Text("Hello World! \(counter)")
        .background(colors.randomElement() ??.blue)
```

© Jayant Varma 2019
J. Varma, *SwiftUI for Absolute Beginners*, https://doi.org/10.1007/978-1-4842-5516-2_11

```
.onReceive(timer) { _ in
    self.counter += 1
}
}
```

Note   To see how SwiftUI works on binding, remove the counter from the Text element and see despite the timer running, there is no change or screen update.

Modifying Content: Styles

We can also create styles like working with Style Sheets; these styles are basically modifiers. We can take advantage of *ViewModifiers* that allow us to create a set of modifiers that we can classify as a style:

```
struct ErrorHeadlines: ViewModifier {
    func body(content: Content) -> some View {
        return content
        .padding()
        .font(.largeTitle)
        .foregroundColor(Color.black)
        .shadow(radius: 2)
        .backgroundColor(Color.blue.opacity(0.2))
        .clipShape(RoundedRectangle(cornerRadius: 10))
        .overlay(
            RoundedRectangle(cornerRadius: 10)
            .stroke(Color.black.opacity(0.2), lineWidth: 1)
        )
    }
}
```

And using it to apply it to the text element, we can simply use it as so

```
var body: some View {
    Text("Hello World!")
    .modifier(ErrorHeadlines())
}
```

And now, we have the text displayed with the style that we applied. This would save us from adding all of that code again repeatedly.

Everything Can Be Conditional?

One simple tip with SwiftUI that we can use very effectively is the *ternary* operator, or the Elvis operator as it is also called. This is a simpler and easier replacement for a single if...else statement. It is not only for SwiftUI but can be used in Swift code; in fact, it used to be very popular with C code, but then was removed due to concerns over readability.

The simple way to use it is to have a value or an object applied depending on the condition, so a simple code block that looks like this:

```
if coffee == .hot {
    textColor = .red
} else {
    textColor = .blue
}
```

This can simply be changed into a single line of code as

```
textColor = coffee == .hot ? Color.red : Color.blue
```

We saw that we also used this in SwiftUI declarations in the following manner:

```
Image(systemName: coffee == .hot ? "thermometer.sun" :
                                   "thermometer.snowflake")
```

167

This will display an image with a sun or a snowflake behind the thermometer indicating that the coffee is hot or cold.

Single Source of Truth

The thing that we should always remember is that there needs to be a single source of truth. This allows us to keep all of the UI in sync. If the source of truth is spread, then it will fail, and we can get mismatched UI updates.

The easiest way to keep a single source of truth is to have the source of truth bound to the UI element, generally using a State or Binding, while the element can have its own data for rendering and so on.

Say we want to create a Coffee temperature element that has a switch and allows us to select the type of coffee we want, hot or cold.

For this, we need the switch to have a state so that the `Bool` value of on or off can be used and bound to the switch. This in turn then when rendered sends the value to the Coffee temperature view that renders the hot or cold icon as seen in Figure 11-1.

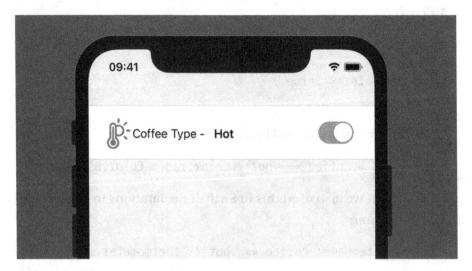

Figure 11-1. *The Hot or Cold coffee selector*

Forms

Creating forms with SwiftUI is very easy; in fact, it is one of the simplest things that developers can create; in the past, creating a form with TableViews or StackViews was very complex and required a lot of plumbing to connect the various elements, their delegates, and so on. Now, creating a form is as simple as wrapping a UI declaration in the Form keyword. It is also recommended to use a NavigationView outside of the Form so that for some elements that might require a NavigationView to select elements, it is provided automatically, like we saw in the case of PickerView earlier in Chapter 3 and also in Figure 11-1.

Model: ViewModel

SwiftUI is based on composition, so just like Lego bricks, we can keep adding more and more functionality by abstracting them into smaller functional units. Instead of having a long element with the modifiers, and so on, we can abstract that into a component. Similarly, we can also use a model and abstract that into a *ViewModel* more fit for purpose than passing around a large model. This can also help to write tests quickly. Say, for example, we have a model that stores desserts and has a lot of information, in our DessertViewModel, we took only the relevant pieces; the easiest way to do so is as follows:

```
let model: DessertViewModel

init(model: Dessert) {
    self.model.name = model.name
    self.model.ratings = model.ratings
    self.model.image = model.imageName
}
```

This helps us create a specific viewModel, and we could further test it as

```
func TestDessertViewModel: XCTestCase {
    let icecream: DessertViewModel = .icecream
    XCAssertEqual(icecream.name, "Ice Cream")
    XCAssertEqual(icecream.ratings, 3)
}
```

Representables

SwiftUI is not available for Objective-C, but we can definitely use Swift and Objective-C Storyboards in SwiftUI. The way to write the wrapper is to use the UIViewRepresentable or the UIViewControllerRepresentable. It requires us to conform to a couple of things, namely, some functions to create and update the view or viewController. Here is a quick example of using a WKWebview from SwiftUI:

```
import WebKit

struct WebViewPage: UIViewRepresentable {
  let theURL: String

  init(_ url: String = "https://www.apple.com") {
      self.theURL = url
  }

  func makeUIView(context: Context) -> WKWebView {
      return WKWebView()
  }

  func updateUIView(_ uiview: WKWebView, context: Context) {
      if let url = URL(string: theURL) {
          let request = URLRequest(url: url)
          uiView.load(request)
      }
  }
}
```

And we can simply use it as

```
var body: some View {
    NavigationView {
        WebViewPage("https://www.microsoft.com")
        .navigationBarTitle("Web Browser")
    }
}
```

This will now present us with a Web Browser that displays the Microsoft webpage as seen in Figure 11-2.

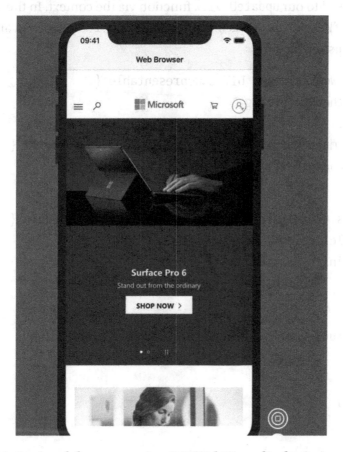

Figure 11-2. *A web browser using WKWebView displaying a web page*

Coordinators and Context

In bridging UIView or UIViewController to SwiftUI, we need to add the
makeUIView and updateUIView functions. The signature of the update
UIView exists a parameter called context, though we have not used this
function nor the context because it did not demonstrate the need to use it
so far. However, say in a case where we want to use delegates and connect
other UIKit functions with the UIView or UIViewController, then we
make use of Coordinators. We use the function makeCoordinator to create
a Coordinator class that can inherit from the appropriate protocols, and
this is passed to our updateUIView function via the context. In the same
example of WKWebView, let us find out when the url starts to load and when
the url finished loading:

```
struct WebViewPage: UIViewRepresentable {
  let theURL: String
  . . .
  func makeCoordinator() -> WebViewPage.Coordinator {
      Coordinator(self)
  }

  class Coordinator: NSObject, WKNavigationDelegate {
      let parent: WebViewPage
      init(_ parent: WebViewPage) {
          self.parent = parent
      }

      func webView(_ webView: WKWebView, didFinish
        navigation: WKNavigation!) {
          //
      }
```

```
    func webView(_ webView: WKWebView,
        didStartProvisionalNavigation navigation:
        WKNavigation!) {
        //
    }

  func webView(_ webView: WKWebView, didFail navigation:
     WKNavigation!, withError error: Error) {
     //
  }

}
```

We can write code to manage what to do at each of these points when the navigation starts, finishes, and has an error. If we connect it with Combine or a publisher, we could send the events up the chain to our view.

Combine

This is the reactive library that Apple has included, and we can make use of that to simply get messages from the handlers. This is a sample to demonstrate the usage, and for more details and learning Combine, a book on Combine would be a better source:

```
enum WebEvent {
    case start, finish, failure(Error)
}

struct WebViewPage: UIViewRepresentable {
  let theURL: String
  let triggerEvent = PassthroughSubject<WebEvent, Never>()
  . . .
}
```

We create a passthrough subject publisher that can publish events, and
then in each of the delegate methods, we can send an event as

```
func webView(_ webView: WKWebView, didFinish navigation:
WKNavigation!) {
    parent.triggerEvent.send(.finish)
}

func webView(_ webView: WKWebView, didStartProvisional
Navigation navigation: WKNavigation!) {
    parent.triggerEvent.send(.start)
}

func webView(_ webView: WKWebView, didFail navigation:
WKNavigation!, withError error: Error) {
    parent.triggerEvent.send(.failure(error))
}
```

And in the View struct, we can subscribe to this and get the
values or bind it with a variable and display it on the UI as seen in the
following code:

```
var body: some View {
    let webPage = WebViewPage("https://www.microsoft.com")

    webPage
    .onReceive(webPage.triggerEvent) { event in
        print("Got : \(event)")
    }
}
```

Adding DebugPrint

When using the SwiftUI views, it is a bit daunting to print the information to the debug console. There is an easier way to do so. We can simply create an extension on the View protocol and add a function called debugPrint like the following:

```
extension View {
    func debugPrint(_ params: Any …) -> Self {
        print(params)
        return self
    }
}
```

Now, this can be used to debug values like the following:

```
struct MyDebugView: View {
    @State private var toggleValue = false

    var body: some View {
        Toggle(isOn: $toggleVlaue) {
            Text("Toggle a value")
        }
        .debugPrint(toggleValue)
    }
}
```

Adding Comments

Taking a page from the preceding debugPrint example, we can create a comment function that allows us to keep the comments in the code as human readable and not interfere with the SwiftUI code at all. This has the advantage that it is part of your binary when compiled, unlike the comments using double slash // or the /* */ comment blocks that are disregarded:

```
extension View {
    func comment(_ comment: String) -> Self {
        return self
    }
}
```

Now using it is as simple as

```
var body: some View {
    VStack {
        Text("Hello World!")
        .comment("Introductory Text here")
    }
}
```

Create Grids

There are times when we might want to create lines for guides, or a grid or some sort of layout; the easiest way to create lines is using the Divider() element as can be seen in Figure 11-3:

```
struct GridView: View {
    var body: some View {
        ZStack {
            VStack(alignment: .center, spacing: 50) {
                ForEach(0..<25) { _ in
                    Divider()
                }
            }
```

```
                HStack(alignment: .center, spacing: 50) {
                    ForEach(0..<25) { _ in
                        Divider()
                    }
                }
            }
        }
    }
```

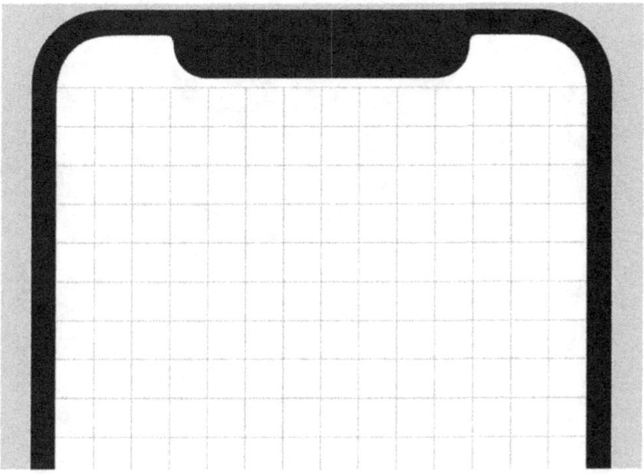

***Figure 11-3.** The grid view on the device using Divider()*

We can also accurately estimate the number of Divider elements that we want to be displayed by calculating that using the `UIScreen.main.bounds` and the expected grid size. This grid could be further extended to create a bitmap editor, where tapping could set a tile on or off.

Summary

This is an exciting technology, and just as Swift has been evolving, SwiftUI will also evolve. This means that things will change before they settle down onto something. The true power of this can be harnessed by using SwiftUI with Combine. There will be a lot more examples included with the source code to refer to. Congratulations on being an early adopter and taking the plunge into learning. All the best in this journey and have fun.

Index

Printed in the United States
By Bookmasters